Advance praise for

Guide to Sea Kayaking
in Southeast Alaska

"Howard provides thorough and accurate pre-trip information coupled with alluring descriptions—and does so without betraying the wonders of discovery. This is an excellent source for paddling southeast Alaska."
    —Tom Watson, Owner, Wavetamer Kayaking, Kodiak, Alaska

"*Guide to Sea Kayaking in Southeast Alaska* is a great starting point for planning your trip in one of the most beautiful places in North America. The information is easy to follow and well organized."
    —Dena Foltz, Managing Editor, *River Magazine*

Help Us Keep This Guide Up to Date

Every effort has been made by the author and editors to make this guide as accurate and useful as possible. However, many things can change after a guide is published—new information becomes available, phone numbers change, hiking trails are rerouted, and so on.

We would love to hear from you concerning your experiences with this guide and how you feel it could be made better and kept up to date. While we may not be able to respond to all comments and suggestions, we'll take them to heart and we'll also make certain to share them with the author. Please send your comments and suggestions to the following address:

The Globe Pequot Press
Reader Response/Editorial Department
P.O. Box 833
Old Saybrook, CT 06475

Or you may e-mail us at:

editorial@globe-pequot.com

Thanks for your input, and happy travels!

Regional Sea Kayaking Series

Guide to Sea Kayaking in Southeast Alaska

The Best Day Trips and Tours from Misty Fjords to Glacier Bay

by

Jim Howard

Old Saybrook, Connecticut

Cover design: Adam Schwartzman
Text design: Casey Shain
Cover photograph: Chris Noble/©Tony Stone Imagess
Map design: Mary Ballachino
Interior photos: Jim Howard

Library of Congress Cataloging-in-Publication Data
Howard, Jim (James D.)
   Guide to sea kayaking in southeast Alaska: the best day trips and tours from Misty Fjords to Glacier Bay/by Jim Howard.—1st ed.
     p.   cm.—(Regional sea kayaking series)
   Includes bibliographical references (p.) and index.
   ISBN 0-7627-0409-8
   1. Sea kayaking—Alaska Guidebooks. 2. Alaska Guidebooks.
I. Title.   II. Title: Best day trips and tours from Misty Fjords to Glacier Bay.   III. Series.
GV788.5.H69 1999
917.98' 20451—dc21   99-21795
                                                                      CIP

Manufactured in the United States of America
First Edition/First Printing

For Andrea

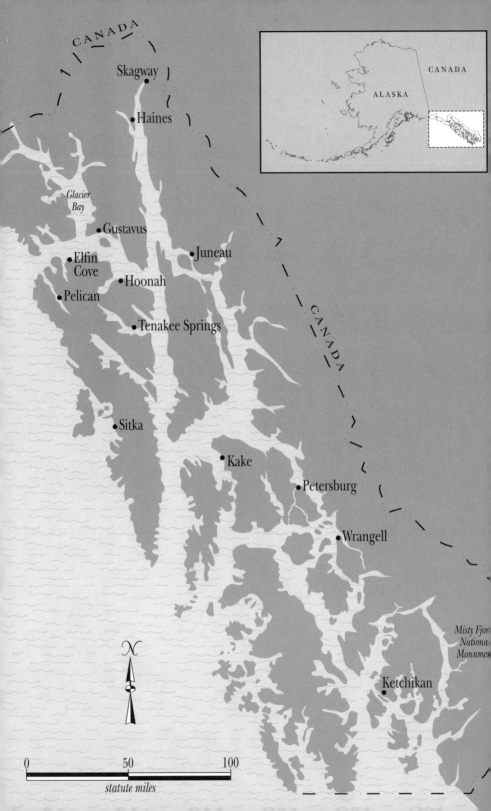

Contents

Acknowledgments

Particular thanks for logistic support over the past four summers goes to Jean and Ken Kemmerer of Ketchikan. Sue Warner, Ken Leghorn, and Karen and Jeff Wilson of Juneau offered the hospitality of their homes on several occasions, as did John Heddon of Sitka and Peggy McDonald and Dennis Montgomery of Gull Cove. Jerry and Sandy Fiscus found storage space for my car and also served as a much needed mail drop in Juneau. Marg Clabby, Eric Hummer, Geoff Gross, Kim Kirby, and Greg Thomas, all of Ketchikan, gave lots of counsel and advice. Scott Roberge of Petersburg generously invited me along on one of his great Stikine River trips. Ned Rozbicki and Heidi Hanson of Haines were unstinting with their time and knowledge of kayaking in Lynn Canal. Linda Frame and Lindy Dickson made my trips to Pelican a lot of fun. Scott Brylinsky graciously took me kayaking for a day in Sitka Sound. Pamela Miedtke and Rusty Owen on *Seawolf* handed me coffee and homemade coffeecake one day while I was paddling across the middle of Glacier Bay. Karen Brand of the U.S. Forest Service in Ketchikan gave me a lot of valuable kayaking information for Misty Fjords National Monument.

Although I take responsibility for what I have written, I appreciate very much the comments on various parts of the manuscript by Andrea Novicki, Kim Kirby, Greg Thomas, Scott Roberge, Ned Rozbicki, Dennis Montgomery, Peggy McDonald, Ken Leghorn, Sue Warner, Scott Brylinsky, Linda Frame, and Melanie Heacox.

Libraries in Ketchikan, Juneau, and Sitka provided work space and Internet access in the summer of 1998. The Harvard University Map Collection offered generous access to their holdings.

Introduction

Once your paddle dips into the chilly waters of Southeast Alaska you are part of an enchanting, dynamic adventure. Each moment is a kaleidoscope of sight and sound that includes the sky, sea, mountains, glaciers, old-growth forests, and a menagerie of birds and beasts. I know of nowhere else on Earth with more compelling beauty and grandeur or where it is possible for both novice and veteran paddlers to experience such an intense wilderness encounter. Sea kayaking in Southeast Alaska is, in a word, *fantastic.*

How This Book Is Organized

The first part of this book, Kayaking Southeast Alaska, presents "tooling up" information for Southeast Alaska kayaking. Each section has a lot of who, what, when, where, and why things to make trip planning easier. They will save you time, money, and mistakes.

The individual routes that make up the second part are a variety of trips originating from nine different geographic locations. This approach reflects the realities of transportation. Southeast Alaska is not like many other places in the world where you can often drive somewhere, off-load your boat, and paddle away. Here the "get to" locations are limited to where the ferries and airlines go.

Finally the appendixes provide information most kayakers will find essential to a successful trip. Most important is Appendix 1, Kayaking Services in Southeast Alaska, a list of the various kayak services, including tour options, rentals, transport services, and Web sites. Other appendixes include cabin rental information, kayaking map sources, reference books, and miscellaneous addresses.

Why These Specific Trips?

The trips in this book were suggested by my experiences. I have paddled almost all of them at least once, and some of them two or three times. If this is your first time kayaking Southeast Alaska, I think you will enjoy any of the trips described. For future trips—and be assured you will want to return—the suggested itineraries can be incorporated into other adventures that you craft yourself. There is an unlimited number of other trips that could be proposed as well, and if you want to modify one of my suggestions, go to it. Fear not, it is pretty difficult to have a "bad" kayak trip in Southeast Alaska.

I make apologies to readers who are disappointed that I have left out one or more of their preferred trips, and also to those who are angry because I *have* included one of their favorites.

What Is Experience & How Do You Get It?

The question of experience is a catch-22. The only way you become experienced is to get out there and do it. If you are a novice paddler who wants to get experience but the book says, "This trip is only for experienced kayakers," take heart. Quite honestly every trip in this book *could* be paddled by most novice paddlers in near perfect weather. It is also true that every trip here *could* turn into a Donnybrook for most any paddler if the weather turns really sour. If kayaking is new for you, go with a guide or experienced friend or pick the less rigorous excursions as you build up your kayaking resume.

As part of the Globe Pequot Regional Kayaking series, this book uses the terms *Beginner, Intermediate,* and *Advanced* in trip ratings. A Beginner is someone who is really new to the game but has paddled a few hours under the supervision of a guide, teacher, or experienced friend. I am probably more liberal in my use of Beginner than others because I trust you to have a good solid chunk of common sense and self-preservation. Intermediate means you have paddled numerous times under a variety of conditions but probably not in Alaska. An Advanced kayaker is someone with a lot of kayaking experience under a wide variety of conditions and preferably some previous time paddling in Alaska.

My advice to any kayaker is to have plenty of time and to take a very conservative approach whenever setting off on a trip. If the situation becomes difficult, be ready to stop and wait for things to improve. Most kayak accidents could have been prevented if the folks involved had simply stopped when they saw that conditions were deteriorating.

Caveats

- I have done my best to accurately describe the trips in this book and to render useful maps. However mistakes and omissions may exist.

- The sketch maps in this book are for reference purposes only. *They are not for navigation.*

- Please remember that at all times you will be paddling in cold water. The maximum summer water temperature is typically 45 to 55 degrees Fahrenheit; in glacial fjords it is 34 to 40 degrees Fahrenheit. At these temperatures exhaustion or unconsciousness occurs in fifteen to sixty minutes and expected time of survival is thirty minutes to about two hours.

- Before setting out on any kayak trip in Alaska, obtain an appropriate weather forecast, have the necessary maps or charts, leave a float plan with a friend or a local harbormaster, and be sure your equipment and gear is appropriate and in good condition (as described in the introductory section of the book). I encourage all novice kayakers and most others who are paddling here for the first time to consider taking part in an organized excursion.

  Happy paddling.

Kayaking Southeast Alaska

Alaska Is Different

Kayaking attitudes developed in less rigorous places don't work the same way in Alaska. What may be a suggestion elsewhere is often hard-won advice here.

Before my first trip north, a veteran of the area advised me that in Alaska a decision is often a commitment. The advice was good. As a kayaker you are commonly on your own. Within minutes of leaving even the largest city, you are usually in a remote place. In the absence of telephones, numbers like 911 lose their significance.

Logistics

Transportation: Getting to Southeast Alaska

Southeast Alaska is an island world. Most towns are on islands, and no roads or bridges from the mainland reach the islands. Consequently you travel by water or by air. This means getting to Southeast Alaska on Alaska Airlines through Seattle or on the Alaska Marine Highway System (AMHS) ferry from Bellingham, Washington (see Table 1). Once in Southeast Alaska, on-going travel is by ferry, airplane, floatplane, powerboat, or by paddling.

ON YOUR WAY

Kayakers who travel by Alaska Airlines either bring a folding kayak or arrange for a rental kayak at their destination. Those coming north on the Alaska Marine Highway System (AMHS) ferry have more options. They can bring a hardshell or folding kayak with them and travel as a "walk-on" or bring a vehicle. Walk-ons pay an extra but not outrageous charge for bringing a hardshell kayak on the ferry. Folding kayaks can

TABLE 1 *Transportation to the main Southeast Alaska towns*

Town	Alaska Airlines*	AMHS	Auk Nu Ferry	Road
Gustavus/ Glacier Bay	✔		✔	
Haines		✔	✔	✔
Hoonah		✔		
Juneau	✔	✔		
Kake		✔		
Ketchikan	✔	✔		
Pelican		✔		
Petersburg	✔	✔		
Sitka	✔	✔		
Tenakee Springs		✔		
Wrangell	✔	✔		

Small commercial planes and/or floatplanes also visit most of these locations.

travel as luggage. With a car you can usually stash the boat on top for no extra charge.

Here are some 1999 *one-way* ferry charges:

Bellingham, Washington to	Ketchikan	Juneau	Sitka
single adult passenger	$164	$226	$208
charge for kayak	$28	$38	$35
vehicle up to 15 feet	$374	$534	$473

Taking a car to Alaska is expensive. If your main purpose for going to Alaska is to kayak, there is really is no good reason to bring a car. There are few roads in Southeast Alaska, and it will be cheaper to leave the car at home or store it in Bellingham.

The Washington to Alaska ferry makes one round-trip each week throughout the year and arrives and departs Bellingham on Friday. During some weeks in the summer, there is an additional ferry. The trip route is as follows: Bellingham, Ketchikan, Wrangell, Petersburg, Juneau, Haines, Skagway, Haines, Juneau, Sitka, Petersburg, Wrangell, Ketchikan, Bellingham. Typical times from Bellingham are thirty-six hours to Ketchikan and fifty hours to Juneau.

Other AMHS ferries connect to other towns as listed in Table 1. Note that Gustavus, which is the gateway to Glacier Bay, is served by the Auk Nu ferry, which does not carry cars but does allow kayaks. All of the AMHS ferries carry vehicles, but there is no vehicle off loading at Tenakee Springs or Pelican. If you are going to Elfin Cove you'll have to fly, it is only served by floatplane.

The AMHS ferry service also operates between Prince Rupert, British Columbia, and Southeast Alaska. However, during the summers of 1996 and 1997, that service was abruptly interrupted for extended periods of time by protesters involved in Canada-U.S. fishing disputes. Be forewarned and check out the fishy political situation before committing to that route.

TRAVELING THE ALASKA MARINE HIGHWAY SYSTEM (AMHS)

Getting to and around Southeast Alaska on the "blue canoes" of the AMHS is a lot more than just convenient transportation. It is nearly nonstop scenic travel in summer when it is light as much as eighteen hours a day.

Don't expect the ferry to Alaska to offer huge savings over flying. In fact it sometimes costs more than discount airfares. But hey, you're on vacation, right? Getting there is part of being there. On the ferry you will meet an interesting cross-section of fellow travelers. You will be with folks heading north to crew on fishing boats or to work for the summer in a cannery, college students who have jobs in the tourist industry, World War II veterans going back to visit places they haven't seen in half a century, Native Americans on their way home, and a wonderful enthusiastic assemblage of tourists of all ages, races, and economic levels.

All of the AMHS ships have large observations salons, restaurants, and/or snack bars. It is possible to have a stateroom, but it is a lot more fun and free to simply set up your tent on deck and camp out. No tent? No problem! There is a solarium deck where you can lay out your sleeping bag on a reclining deck chair or on deck. Cooking is not allowed but you can bring any cold food along that you want. Most ferries have hot showers.

Kayaking Southeast Alaska

Once You Are There

After you arrive at your location as listed in Table 1, you may not yet be at the specific place from which you want to kayak. For example, Misty Fjords National Monument is some 40 miles from Ketchikan. You can kayak there, but this adds at least two days to each end of the main attraction of the excursion and not everyone wants to do this. Similar examples exist for Tracy and Endicott Arms near Juneau, for the East and West Arms of Glacier Bay, and a few other places.

To get from a ferry/airline terminal to exactly where you want to begin paddling, you can use a kayak transportation service, which you can arrange for on your own or through a kayak rental company. These support services are either (a) small boats that will carry kayakers most any place, or (b) tourist excursion boats that will off-load or meet paddlers at specific locations on a daily schedule. (See Appendix 1 for a list of kayak transport services.)

It is possible to travel most anywhere in Southeast Alaska by float-plane if you have a folding kayak. Some floatplane services with large aircraft will transport hardshell kayaks inside the plane, but this is very expensive.

GETTING AROUND IN TOWN

Southeast Alaska is geared to tourists and visitors. Consequently there is good public transportation available at the ferry and airline terminals. Also because the towns are small, distances are not great. For those coming to Alaska to kayak, it is seldom necessary to rent a car. If you are staying in town, you are invariably within walking distance of where you want to go, or else there is public transportation available. Often businesses that rent kayaks are located on the water, or they can arrange transport for you and your kayak. Some of them will even pick you up at the airport or ferry terminal if they have advanced warning. Most campgrounds are several miles from town, but hitchhiking is popular and acceptable in Alaska. If you want to you can launch your kayak from any ferry terminal in Southeast Alaska.

ACCOMMODATIONS

Alaska tends to be more expensive than a lot of places in the "lower 48," and it has fewer budget or bargain accommodations. (Appendix 4 lists guidebooks that describe a range of accommodations and restaurants in each town.) It is a good idea to book rooms in advance. There are youth hostels and campgrounds in Ketchikan, Juneau, Sitka, and Haines and a campground and dormitory at Glacier Bay.

Ways to Kayak Southeast Alaska

There are a number of ways to kayak Southeast Alaska. You may want to join an arranged trip or organize things for yourself. Many who make their first kayak trip to Alaska benefit from joining a guided kayak excursion rather than going on their own. Even experienced paddlers should consider this option if they are not used to glacier-cold water, tide ranges in excess of 20 feet, wilderness camping, and travel through vast uninhabited areas.

Pros & Cons

Trying to organize a kayak trip from a distance can be daunting. For those with limited time or interest in logistics, a kayaking adventure led by experts is highly recommended. On a guided trip your main

Kayaking Southeast Alaska

responsibility is to show up on time. Scheduling, itinerary, logistics, equipment, camping gear, food, and cooking are all taken care of for you. Trips are arranged to assure interesting, safe, environmentally responsible, wilderness kayaking, and camping. Your guide knows where to go to get the maximum out of a trip. No one on his or her own can possibly see and do as much in an equal period of time on a first trip to Alaska.

Consider too the advantages of the less strenuous approach provided by an arranged trip. If you or someone in your group has trepidations about Alaska camping, a guided trip is a good choice. Macho males or females with reluctant spouses or apprehensive children should take particular note of this point. A good experience the first time out is an ideal way to develop family interest in kayak-camping.

On the other hand, guided trips will not appeal to everyone. The cost of a guided trip is probably higher than if you are traveling on your own. Groups may move slower than you prefer. Usually a guided trip will include less paddling and fewer miles covered each day than if you were traveling by yourself.

If you yearn for independence, enjoy being in control of your adventures, want the thrill of discovering things on your own, and especially if you are on a limited budget, then independent kayaking is the better choice.

G U I D E D   T R I P S

On most guided trips nearly everything is furnished except your personal gear, camera, film, sunglasses, etc. Some companies supply or rent boots and rain gear. All will furnish you with a list of items to bring with you—along with the admonition to not bring too much.

There are not a lot of companies offering guided kayaking trips in Alaska . . . but there are enough. All of the trips are excellent, and each company offers some unique features. There are four kinds of "guided" kayak trips in Southeast Alaska: scheduled trips, guided trips, sailing-kayaking tours, and bed-and-breakfast kayaking. (Appendix 1 lists a variety of companies offering guided kayaking.)

Scheduled Trips. Scheduled trips offer prearranged itineraries to specific places. They appeal especially to those who have never been to Alaska or are too busy to do much pretrip research and planning. Trips are highly organized but maintain a friendly intimacy because they are limited to ten people.

Designed Guided Trips. Organizers offer guided trips for groups as small as two people or as large as ten. They are personalized kayak trips and focus specifically on what you and your group wants to see and do. If you are mainly interested in paddling among humpback whales, or you want to get intimate with glaciers, that is the trip you will have. Kayaking can also be combined with hiking, bird watching, fishing, or even berry picking.

SAILING-KAYAKING TOURS

The term *sailing* is used here in its broadest sense because the vessels are either powerboats or sailboats that end up motoring most of the time. These trips provide a comfort-able mobile base with accommodations, shower, and home-cooked meals. As you might suspect the smaller the vessel, the more personal the trip will be. If the vessel carries more than fifteen people, you are on more of a tour than an adventure.

B & B KAYAKING

Bed-and-breakfast accomodations combined with paddling is a new approach that is proving popular. You spend each day paddling solo or with a guide and then end up in the evening at a comfortable B&B. A variation is to stay at a bed-and-breakfast and make daily excursions.

Kayaking on Your Own

Every year a lot of folks travel to Southeast Alaska to spend days, weeks, or months paddling on self-led adventures. This is easy enough to do provided you have the right gear and are realistic about times and distances. Much of this book is devoted to advising you on this kind of kayaking.

Try to arrive in Alaska with everything you need if you are planning to paddle and camp for several days or weeks. If however you forgot something, Alaska is not outer space. Juneau, Ketchikan, and Sitka offer provisioning and stores for any kind of paddling or camping equipment you could want. Furthermore UPS and FedEx are widely available.

GUIDES

In my experience Alaska kayak guides are outstanding folks. They are knowledgeable, experienced, unflappable, safety conscious, environmentally sensitive, responsible, thoughtful, and endowed with incredible patience and good humor. A lot of them are excellent cooks as well. These women and men have a lot of responsibility to deal with day and night on an excursion. Decisions and game plans are constantly changing in a business where nothing is ever the same from trip to trip or day to day.

The most responsible companies pay their guides a respectable wage, but this is not a get-rich kind of a job. You can be sure that kayak guides are there because they want to be and because of their love of Alaska, which is substantiated by the fact that some Alaska Discovery guides have been with the company more than 20 years.

KAYAK RENTALS

Kayak rentals are available in the larger towns and at Glacier Bay National Park (see Appendix 1). But be sure to make reservations in advance. Sometimes it is possible to just show up and get the kayak you want, but in midsummer demand often exceeds supply.

Rental rates vary slightly, but there is not enough competition to make one company less expensive than another. Responsible rental companies will want to know how much paddling experience you have and will require all renters to take part in a thorough orientation with emphasis on safety and survival. If you or anyone in your group is new to kayaking, some rental companies offer training classes.

Don't expect rental kayaks to be the latest in fancy or high-tech equipment. These are tough, stable boats that can take a lot of hard use. Rental companies have more doubles than singles so if you are after a single make an early reservation. Always ask if the kayak is plastic or fiberglass. For day trips it doesn't make much difference. For week-long kayak-camping, a glass boat will carry more gear and supplies.

Find out exactly what equipment comes with your kayak rental when making a reservation. At a minimum it should include a spray skirt, pump, life jacket/personal flotation device (PFD), sponge, and a

paddle. Signaling devices including a whistle and flares may or may not be provided. Some companies rent boots and rain gear for an additional charge. Some provide or sell maps.

Depending on where and how long you are paddling, you may want to consider renting a VHF radio, compass, and other specific gear if that is an option. I recommend having an extra paddle for a single or double and perhaps two for a group of four or five boats. If you rent from a company that is not on the water, or if you want to start your trip at some specific place, ask about the charges for transpor-tation to and from a launch point.

For a week or two, the cost of renting versus the hassle of bringing your own boat to Alaska may tip the scales toward a rental. All companies have weekly and longer rates that are a signigicant iimprovement on the daily rates. If you are renting longer than three weeks, it begins to get pricey, and you may decide to bring your own kayak or to buy a new or used one in Alaska.

Kayaking Southeast Alaska

In Southeast Alaska you will meet single-handers, couples, and groups of kayakers. Each option has its plus and minus points. It is human nature to be gregarious and to enjoy sharing experiences. Couples and larger groups can carry more gear and food for longer trips; more people means the campsite tasks can be passed around.

But just as some people find joy in sharing experiences, others find pleasure in making discoveries alone. Solo travel is certainly realistic in Southeast Alaska. The advantages of solo kayaking are the obvious ones of solitude, freedom to make spontaneous decisions, and the opportunity to do pretty much what you want to do. Some kayak alone because it is the best way to observe and photograph wildlife.

P L A N   A H E A D

Going on a guided tour or planning to rent equipment in Alaska? Get cracking early on making your reservations. Alaska kayaking fever seems to hit a lot of "lower 48" folks about the time they notice the crocus springing up and lilacs bursting into bloom. A few weeks earlier would have been better. Juggling airline reservations, booking for a guided trip, or reserving rental gear can get pretty intense if you wait till the last minute.

Trip Planning

Duration of Kayaking Trips

H A L F -   &   F U L L - D A Y   G U I D E D   T R I P S

Guided trips of a day or less can be made pretty much spur of the moment in Ketchikan, Petersburg, Juneau, Haines, Pelican, Sitka, or at Bartlett Cove in Glacier Bay. A lot of people traveling in Alaska on cruise ships get their first taste of sea kayaking by taking a guided trip for a few hours. These quickies usually track in and around the harbors while your guide introduces you to some Alaskan history and scenery. This type of trip is a gentle, benign adventure under the watchful eye of your guide. If you have the choice, opt for a tour that takes out groups of ten or fewer kayaks.

ON-YOUR-OWN DAY TRIPS

There are a lot of possibilities for on-your-own day trips in Alaska. Try to plan trips away from the main harbors. After all you did not come to Alaska to dodge fishing boats and smell diesel fumes. Some excellent day trips can be made from campgrounds in Ketchikan, Sitka, and Bartlett Cove at Glacier Bay National Park.

If you take the ferry to one of the small towns, you can set up a camp and kayak day trips from there. In Ketchikan, Pelican, Gustavus, and at Elfin Cove, there are opportunities to make day trips while enjoying the comfort of a B&B. In Sitka, Ketchikan, and Juneau, you can arrange to have your kayak rental company take you by truck away from the busy harbor to a put-in location and later pick you up at that or another location.

KAYAK-CAMPING TRIPS

Kayak-camping trips are what sea kayaking is really about in Southeast Alaska, and they include a tremendous range of options in terms of where to go, how to go, and how long to go for. In the broadest sense these trips include everything from overnighters to week- and even monthlong or longer excursions. Regardless of duration if you are wilderness camping, you really must have the proper kayaking and camping gear.

For those on their own, trips of two or three days are certainly possible, but most folks opt for a minimum of five days. The unpredictability and fickleness of the weather makes this a good idea. You can almost be sure that at least one day in the week will be rainy and/or windy. Rain need not keep you from paddling, but if it happens to be combined with gusty conditions, a day in camp will be a wise and easy decision to make—especially if you remembered to bring along a good book and a sufficient stash of chocolate! If a layover day becomes necessary on a two or three day trip, the impact is pretty significant. If it interrupts a longer adventure, it will seem less devastating. Consider too that it takes a while to settle into and become comfortable with the rhythm of Alaska wilderness kayaking. If your time is too short, you will just be getting into the swing of things when it is time to head home.

My recommendation for any kayak-camping trip is to take a minimum of five days. If you use a kayak transportation service or if you go with a guided service, you can expect that at least half of the first and last days will be spent being transported by boat or floatplane. Realistically that means you will only be paddling for three or four days. If you are a typical paddler-camper, reserve one of those days for hiking, just hanging out in camp, or as an offering to the weather god. With this schedule you can have a nice—albeit short—trip in a variety of locations. Trips of seven to ten days are *much* to be preferred.

Beyond ten days? Personally I prefer trips of two to three weeks, but that is more time than a lot of folks can afford to spend in the great outdoors. Those who do choose a longer stay will find plenty of opportunities for extended trips (I will mention some in the chapters ahead).

Best Time for Kayaking

May, June, July, and August are the most popular kayaking months. May is a great time to see ducks and bears. It is still pretty cool, and in upper Glacier Bay there may be snow down to the water. But this is the time when you will have a lot of wilderness to yourself. June is popular because it is the time of least precipitation, and the tourist crowds are only beginning to arrive. July and August are the best times for seeing whales, for berry picking and for salmon fishing; it is also an opportune time to see bears harvesting fish. September is rather "iffy"; usually there are two weeks of beautiful weather and two weeks of horrible blowy, rainy days. The problem is no one knows which two will happen when.

The Weather

TEMPERATURE

Summer temperatures are typically cool by day and cooler by night, making for enjoyable paddling and great sleeping as long as you are warm and dry. Expect daytime averages to be in the lower 60s and nights in the 50s. Some days the temperature can climb into the 70s and occasionally into the 80s. If you come in May, you can lower those average figures by five or ten degrees. Temperatures are noticeably cooler in the vicinity of glaciers and especially so if the wind is blowing off the ice. (Most of the time temperatures will range as shown in Table 2.)

TABLE 2 *Typical Summer Temperature*

	May	June	July	August
Ketchikan area	57/49*	62/55	65/58	66/59
Sitka area	53/47	58/52	61/56	62/57
Juneau area	55/47	61/53	64/56	62/55
Glacier Bay	53/45	59/52	62/55	61/54

* Highs/lows (degrees F).

PRECIPITATION

So now it is time to talk about rain. Southeast Alaska is a rain forest, and there is only one way you can earn that designation. All those beautiful old-growth trees surrounded by fragrant, soft, mossy, flower-covered forest floors, and all those delicious berries on the understory shrubs are due to . . . rain. Consider too that one of Alaska's greatest treasures—Misty Fjords—is misty for just one reason.

TABLE 3 *"Typical" Rainfall Averages (in inches)*

	May	June	July	August
Ketchikan area	9.1	7.4	7.8	10.6
Sitka area	4.8	3.7	4.4	6.9
Juneau area	3.5	3.0	4.0	5.1
Glacier Bay	1.9	1.9	2.7	3.6

Kayaking Southeast Alaska

How much does it rain in Southeast Alaska? Guidebooks discuss at length how this or that town gets more or less rain than its neighbor. The facts are that it rains a lot most everywhere. However, like Shakespeare's "quality of mercy" analogy, it "droppeth" gently from heaven. It is a mostly soft, frequent rain. It is nice friendly rain and not a problem if you wear proper rain gear. So expect rain, be prepared for rain, and learn to enjoy rain. (Table 3 gives you an idea of average amounts of rainfall.) On the other hand don't be disappointed if you are unlucky and hit a stretch of continuous sunny days. It happens.

I recall some of my most enjoyable kayaking days have been in the rain when the water surface is often like glass. And some of my most memorable photographs have gray as their distinctive tone.

W I N D

It is difficult to summarize and write about Southeast Alaska winds. Looking only at the National Oceanic and Atmospheric Administration (NOAA) Weather Service data spread out in front of me, things look rather grim. In fact experience tells me they are not. I certainly can recall days when whitecaps on the water and prudence in my soul told me to stay camped for another day. But I recall many more times when I slipped along on glassy smooth surfaces or paddled along on a rippled

surface with just enough breeze to allow the spruce boughs overhead a quiet conversation.

Most often the summer wind is from the southeast with wind speeds of less than 10 knots. But the winds can and do shift around the compass, and in places open to the Pacific, such as Cross Sound and Icy Strait, a northwest and westerly component can be significant.

In most cases—except when a front is galloping through—the day's wind comes up in the afternoon. This gives you the option to get going early in the morning and put most of the day's paddle miles behind you by noon. The generally southeast winds also give the clear message that trips that move from south to north will generally be easier. When fronts do occur, they are commonly one-day affairs associated with rain. Such systems will now and then persist for two or even three days.

WEATHER FORECASTS

Throughout this book I mention the importance of obtaining a weather forecast before setting out on any kayaking trip. There are a number of ways to do this. The easiest is from the weather channel found on most VHF radios. Some of the small boat harbors in Alaska have weather forecast radios at the dock, and you can always get a forecast at a harbormaster's office. If there is a telephone nearby, the National Weather Service offers a toll-free phone forecast (1–800–472–0391). The Coast Guard broadcasts a weather forecast twice a day. This is announced on VHF Channel 16 and broadcast on Channel 22. National Public Radio stations on FM can be heard in every town in Southeast Alaska, and they give frequent weather forecasts and summaries.

Shipping & Mailing

If you want to lighten the travel load, it is possible to ship some of your gear north ahead of time. The U.S. postal service is in every little town, and post office supervisors in Alaska tend to be understanding about holding general delivery packages—especially if you write them a letter or give them a phone call. It doesn't hurt to also write a note on the box next to the address saying that you are kayaking and giving an approximate date when you expect to arrive.

When I am planning long trips, I prepare packages with food (and books) that I leave with a friend. Then when I am about to start paddling to a new destination—perhaps three weeks ahead—I call and ask my friend to send the package to me c/o General Delivery at my destination.

Daily Routine

Before my first trip to Alaska, I wondered what a kayak trip would be like. If you have similar thoughts, here are some examples of my experiences: The days are long. There is so much daylight that you may tend to sleep less and enjoy more. When you are paddling it pays to go with the flow and use the ebb and flood of the tides to speed you on your way. Consequently a paddling day can sometimes begin at 4:00 or 5:00 A.M. to catch a favorable tide and calm waters. If you are not a "morning person," this may sound horrendous. But early mornings are perfect times to observe wildlife and enjoy a magnificent sunrise. And if you begin early, you can quit early as well.

It typically takes about an hour to break camp, load the boat, and be on the way. Stopping and setting up camp takes about the same time. As I paddle I generally do a lot of exploring along the way and poke into small coves and bays. It is nice to hang close to shore because of the opportunity to see more wildlife. I make a few stops along the way just to keep my legs from getting too lazy. I have no set number of miles or hours to go each day. Rather I select a potential destination and two or three alternatives. If I find a spot that especially appeals to me, I will make that my campsite. Some days I do as little as 4 or 5 miles, and other times I have done 25 or 30 miles with a substantial boost from the current. If this is your first trip north and your experience level is average, consider a one-week trip of no more than 40 or 50 miles.

BE REALISTIC

Unrealistic expectations for paddling times and distances are probably the greatest causes of accidents and disappointments when kayaking on your own in Alaska. Unpredictable weather can happen. It is something that comes with the territory. Budget some time in you trip plans for this possibility. Some years the weather is better— or worse—than other years, but the possibility that there will be days when you prefer to stay in camp must always be factored into your planning.

I also have layover days. Two kinds. One when I stay at the same campsite for two or more nights and spend days making short kayak trips, hiking, reading, birding, berry picking, or just relaxing. The other kind of layover day occurs when the weather is not wonderful and needs to be waited out. For either kind of day, it pays to bring along a nice, friendly book.

I don't break camp if there are whitecaps on the water. In my experience it isn't worth the hassle. Other times when a day starts out with harsh weather and then turns nice by midmorning or noon, I often go ahead and get underway. Most important is to budget plenty of extra time so that you are not rushed or feel the need to paddle in marginal conditions.

Kayak Equipment

The Right Boat

At the risk of sounding flippant, I believe the best kayak is the one that works for you. Fiberglass, plastic, and wood boats are seen everywhere, as are the various folding kayaks. What boat you bring north with you doesn't really matter if it is one you are used to and with which you feel comfortable. On the other hand experienced Alaska kayaker Ned Rozbicki of Haines points out the importance of positive buoyancy in the event of capsize in these very cold waters. Watertight bulkheads, sea socks as used in Feathercraft foldables, or sponsons are add-ons very worthy of consideration.

An inflatable kayak surely doesn't get my vote for Alaska paddle-camping, but it is the choice of author Audry Sutherland—and no one is more experienced in cruising the waters of British Colombia and Southeast Alaska than she. But the operant word here is *experienced*. Remember too that Audry Sutherland has customized her boat to fit her needs.

I have no experience in canoeing in Alaska, but I have seen very few canoes in my travels there. In Glacier Bay a couple of years ago, I talked to some experienced Belgian paddlers who had just returned from a three-week trip up bay in folding canoes. They were pretty bummed out with their experience and said they would never do it again with canoes because of windage. But if there are a lot of portages in your plans, a canoe is far better than a kayak.

Boat Equipment

Ancillary kayak gear is pretty much the standard stuff that you have always been told you should have. But in Alaska *should* becomes *must,* and if you have been a bit "gear slack" while paddling in Baja, let me remind you once more that Alaska is different. If you or one of your paddling buddies capsizes in this cold water, it is more than just a reality check, it is a very serious situation. You are immediately in survival mode and racing against the clock. Everything needs to work right.

Minimum Necessities

Following are the items I believe you should absolutely have with you for kayaking in Southeast Alaska.

- **Life jacket (PFD) that is the right size and in good condition**

- **Spray skirt that is fitted to your boat and fits you properly**

- **Pump that you have tested, that is usable from the cockpit, and that is attached to the boat**

- **Sponge**

- **Spare (2-piece) paddle that you can quickly and easily reach from the cockpit**

- **Paddle float and/or sponsons to aid in climbing back aboard from a capsize**

- **Bow and stern lines that can be deployed from the cockpit**

- **Mooring/tow rope that can be used from the cockpit**

- **Signal flares accessible from the cockpit and preferably transportable in a waterproof container in your life jacket**

- **Whistle attached to life jacket**

- **Matches carried in waterproof container in life jacket**

- **Repair kit for emergency patching of kayak, including Aquaseal, duct tape, and whatever else the manufacturer recommends**

- First-aid kit available from the cockpit

- Map compass

- Waterproof see-through map case that ties to boat

If you are renting a kayak, some of this gear will be furnished, but if you have your own equipment and it is in top-notch condition, consider bringing it with you.

Recommended Equipment Options

When it comes to equipment options, things become more opinionated. Some folks may consider the following to be mandatory, while others think them unnecessary:

- Boat compass that mounts on deck and is easy to read from the cockpit

- Strobe for emergency signaling

- VHF handheld radio that operates on AA batteries

- Weather radio (most VHF radios also pick up the weather channels)

- Dry bags for storing all gear, clothing, and food

- Cockpit cover

- Paddle leash (especially if you don't have a spare paddle)

I have kayaked in Southeast Alaska with and without a compass. It is not crucial, but it is handy and reassuring to have. VHF and weather radios are recommended. In a lot of places, however, there is no reception because of the topography. On the other hand if you get in trouble or if you want to alert an approaching boat or ship of your presence, a VHF handheld radio is important. Be sure to keep it waterproof and available. The models that operate on AA battery packs are best. Rechargeables are unreliable because they cannot be recharged in the field.

Dry bags pay off because some water will get into just about any kayak now and then, and salt water does not add anything desirable to camp food. Dry bags are also very easy to suspend from trees, the traditional way of avoiding food loss to critters. Dry bags are available from stores that cater to kayak and canoeing folks. They are expensive but have a long life. If necessary double or triple plastic garbage bags can be used for short trips, but nothing can beat a dry bag.

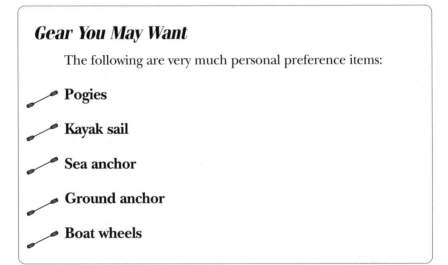

Gear You May Want

The following are very much personal preference items:

- **Pogies**
- **Kayak sail**
- **Sea anchor**
- **Ground anchor**
- **Boat wheels**

I have never used or felt I needed any of these items. Furthermore there is only so much space available, and I would rather carry more food or film than any of the foregoing.

THINGS THAT GO "BEEP"

Some kayakers consider a global positioning system (GPS) and/or an emergency position-indicating radio beacon (EPIRB) essential, but for most of us they are unnecessary. Having spent a dozen years sailing throughout the Pacific Ocean, I am well acquainted with GPSs and EPIRBs, and in that setting I rely on them absolutely. For kayaking in Southeast Alaska, I see no need for them. Landforms here are so prominent that you have to try really hard to get lost. Furthermore precisely plotting positions on a small-scale map carried in a plastic envelope in the cockpit of a kayak is humorous at best. Last summer in Alaska I met two different kayakers who were completely lost, and both were using GPS instead of looking around.

A 406 MHz EPIRB signal connects vessels in distress with a satellite system and will certainly alert the Coast Guard that someone needs help. However I consider them to be too bulky and too expensive for the kind of nearshore paddling that characterizes Southeast Alaska.

Clothing

Form should follow function rather than fashion when it comes to kayak clothing for Alaska. For anything other than a two- or three-hour guided excursion, it is important to have clothing that you can absolutely depend on to keep you warm and dry. First and foremost you should have a totally waterproof jacket. This is a necessity no matter how much kayaking you plan to do, whereas rain pants are optional if you are just doing day trips. The best possible rain gear is the latest version of Gore-Tex, which will keep you absolutely dry. It will be expensive, but for any extended paddling, or hiking for that matter, it is the only way to go. Some of the best jackets for kayaking are those made by Kokotat and Patagonia.

Rain pants for extended kayaking in Southeast Alaska need to be selected with care. Some fabrics are too fragile. You will at some time be sitting on rough rock surfaces so select pants that can take it. If you do find holes or tears developing in any of your rain gear, they can be fixed jiffy quick with Aquaseal—the same stuff that will patch leaking kayaks, torn tents, punctured boots, and probably even broken hearts.

Do you need a wet suit or dry suit for Southeast Alaska kayaking? In my opinion you don't need either. They are inconvenient to get in and out of and turn into a steam bath on warm days, and quite frankly you can really work up a stink in them when paddling. Anyway this is very specialized gear whereas a good Gore-Tex rain jacket and pants can be used for other activities.

Clothing Recommendations

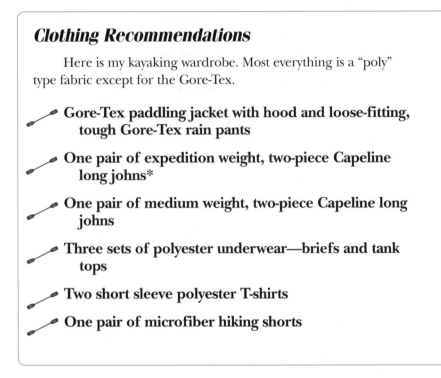

Here is my kayaking wardrobe. Most everything is a "poly" type fabric except for the Gore-Tex.

- **Gore-Tex paddling jacket with hood and loose-fitting, tough Gore-Tex rain pants**

- **One pair of expedition weight, two-piece Capeline long johns***

- **One pair of medium weight, two-piece Capeline long johns**

- **Three sets of polyester underwear—briefs and tank tops**

- **Two short sleeve polyester T-shirts**

- **One pair of microfiber hiking shorts**

Before my first kayaking trip to Alaska, I pondered long and hard as to the proper footwear and even conjured up some innovative ideas that in retrospect bordered on the absurd. All that is really necessary are good rubber or neoprene boots that come up almost to the knee.

Hip boots are not necessary for kayaking and in fact are potentially dangerous. Dive booties will not keep your feet dry, and wet feet are cold feet. Leather hiking boots are better left at home.

The best boot I have found is Alaska's ubiquitous Xtra-Tuff. You will find them anyplace in Alaska that sells sporting goods or commercial fishing supplies. They are strong and comfortable and even work well for short hikes. Be sure and buy a felt sole liner as well, and try on the boot with the liners in.

Other clothing needs depend on how long you plan to kayak and what you can afford. Operant words are *layers* and *wicking*. Sea kayaking need not be a strenuous activity, but it can cause the body to heat up and cool down frequently. Hence you want to be able to add or take off layers of clothing quickly and easily. I have come to consider clothing

- One pair of microfiber lightweight long pants
- Three pairs of polyester socks
- Tevas (sandals)
- Xtra-Tuffs (knee boots)
- Neoprene gloves
- One pair of bicycling gloves
- Polyester watch cap
- Baseball cap

*It is possible to get along with one set of long johns. I carry a spare as a matter of safety. I figure if I ever fall in the water, I will want to change into some warm, dry clothes as quickly as possible.

made from polyester fabrics as the only ones for Alaska kayaking. It wicks moisture away from the body and layers well; it is easy to wash and dries quickly. Polyester comes with a variety of brand names such as Capeline, Duofold, etc.

For the layers over the polyester some folks like synthetic pile such as Polartec fleece or Synchilla. I find it too bulky for kayaking, and so I stick to more layers of polyester.

Camping Gear

If you are kayak-camping in Southeast Alaska, your camping gear is as important as your boat. I can't prove it, but I would bet more people get in trouble because of poor camping equipment than because of poor boat equipment.

Be sure your tent is waterproof and then use it carefully to keep it that way. In Alaska "wet" soon becomes "cold and wet," and hypothermia is next.

Here are my recommendations for the minimum camping gear necessary:

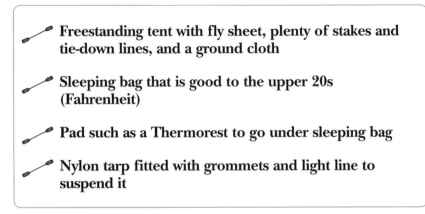

- **Freestanding tent with fly sheet, plenty of stakes and tie-down lines, and a ground cloth**

- **Sleeping bag that is good to the upper 20s (Fahrenheit)**

- **Pad such as a Thermorest to go under sleeping bag**

- **Nylon tarp fitted with grommets and light line to suspend it**

On the subject of tents, the advice is to buy the best you can afford. A freestanding tent is necessary because you may end up in places where there is nothing to tie to.

Don't skimp on tent size. I prefer a three-person tent for solo or double kayaking. You'll appreciate the extra space when you have to spend a day or so waiting out bad weather. Get the lightest weight tent you can consistent with the other important points, but avoid tents made with netting. These are for desert conditions. With a rain fly they will usually keep you reasonably dry for a while, but eventually water will work its way in.

A proper tent will be expensive so follow the manufacturer's recommen-dations for seam sealing and especially for drying and cleaning after your trip. Mildew is a big problem, and manufacturer will not help you out if your tent is badly mildewed.

If you paddle long enough in Southeast Alaska, you will some day have to camp in strong winds. In that circumstance it will be necessary to tie the tent down very securely, using rocks, logs, trees, saplings, and what-have-you as anchors. Be prepared with plenty of line and tent pegs.

I highly recommend a groundcloth; it will add years to the life of your tent floor. Buy one ready-made or save money and make your own from plastic sheeting cut to the same size as the tent floor.

Good sleeping bags are pricey but worth it. In spite of a lot of advice to the contrary, I prefer down bags because they are less bulky and easier to pack. I store mine in a dry bag and have not had a problem with it getting wet.

Kayaking Southeast Alaska

SELECTING A CAMPSITE

Here are some things to keep in mind when deciding where to pitch a tent:

How difficult will it be to get across the intertidal zone with kayak and gear?

Are you well above the high-tide line? Find the last wrack line and check the tide table.

Are you clear of bear trails?

Is there enough room to pitch a tent on a well-drained spot? Even places that appear dry may turn sour in the rain. For example, avoid camping any place where you find skunk cabbage growing—the area can easily become a pond in the rain.

What is the wind situation? If there is heavy wind, you will want to find a protected spot. If there are a lot of no-see-ums (gnats), a breezy point is better.

Is there fresh water near by? This is a convenience but may not be a necessity.

Is the site away from other campers and boat noise?

A sleeping pad is worth the space and weight. The Thermorest brand is reliable. The three-quarter size is sufficient. If you do get a Thermorest, consider also getting the chair conversion kit, which is nice to have for layover days.

A nylon tarp is definitely a should-have item. If your tent develops a leak, a tarp suspended over it will save the day. If your tent is lost, badly damaged, or destroyed, the tarp could save your life. A tarp can provide shade or—more likely—shelter from the rain for cooking or just hanging out. Consider buying a bright color tarp as it might be useful someday as a signaling device.

There is a lot of tempting camping equipment that seems extremely practical or even necessary. Shovels, saws, tables, espresso sets, chairs, etc. are all costly, and they can quickly use up valuable space. Rather than buying and taking them along "in case you need them," consider making the trip without them and keep a record of anything you would like to have along on your next trip.

Galley Gear, Water, & Food

Don't plan on cooking over wood fires in Southeast Alaska unless you are a true survivalist. For a lot of people, wood fires are considered politically incorrect, but that aside it is sometimes impossible to find dry kindling or firewood. An MSR camp stove that can use a variety of liquid fuels is convenient. It is illegal to carry fuel on the airlines, so if you fly it will be necessary to buy fuel when you arrive. It seems like you can always buy some sort of liquid fuel just about anywhere. Propane cylinders are certainly convenient, but what if they are not available at your destination? I use about one liter of white gas per week when traveling by myself. Two people might plan for two liters per week. Cylindrical fuel bottles are better than cans for carrying fuel.

Galley Gear

Weight, reliability, and convenience are considerations when selecting what equipment you need for preparing meals. My cookwear consists of a one-liter and a two-liter pan with lids and a Banks "bake-fry" pan. These three items are the minimum sufficient for one or two people. Other than that I have one of the large Lexan tablespoon and a spatula. The spoon is for mixing, stirring, and eating. The only knife I need is the blade on a Leatherman folding tool. I also carry a small widemouthed thermos, a cup, and a cloth bag coffee filter. Believe it or not that is all the galley gear I have and all I need in the way of cooking gear.

Water

Finding water is rarely a problem in Southeast Alaska. Collecting and treating it however deserves some thought. Giardia is a reality, and the U.S. Forest Service urges all campers to boil, filter, or chemically treat all water collected in the wilderness. When I feel it is necessary to purify, I use a Sweetwater filter, which is quick and easy.

Water bags are convenient for storing and carrying water. Generally they are easy to fill if there is any kind of small rapids or falls. A collapsible plastic bucket is a handy camp item for washing clothes or bodies.

Food

The trade-offs for kayak food are weight, space, convenience, nutrition, and enjoyment. Although I really enjoy cooking and good food, I am a no-frills kayak-camper, and this extends to the foods I eat. Consequently I rely pretty much on freeze-dried camp foods for dinner, nutrition bars or trail mix for lunch, and oatmeal, biscuits, or pancakes for breakfast. It may not be inspiring but it is easy, convenient, and light weight.

For some, creative meals are part of the camping experience. Kayakers who travel in groups, especially those on short excursions, can bring along a more interesting variety of foods. Certainly there are ample opportunities for fishing and crabbing, offering a lot of tasty possibilities. There are a number of interesting plants that are edible and readily available as well. I make an exception to my usual boring food routine during berry time and always take advantage of the salmonberries, blueberries, and red huckleberries that are so abundant and easy to gather.

FOOD STORAGE

For convenience and to save space, I package or repackage all of my food in zip-lock bags, and store these in a dry bag. Dry bags are expensive, and for short trips you can use double garbage bags. If you use them, bring along some extras and be sure to haul out at least as many bags as you haul into the wilderness.

At Glacier Bay the Park Service requires kayakers to use bear-resistant food containers, which they loan at no cost. They are small enough to fit through the hatches on most kayaks. But be forewarned that even though they may be "bear-proof," they are not waterproof. Everything that goes in the bear box needs to be in a Ziploc bag, or the bear box itself should be inside a dry bag.

Matters of Concern

Recognizing Potential Hazards

The key word when discussing the hazards of kayaking is *recognizing*. If you are not aware there is a danger until it is "in your face," it may be too late. Thousands of kayakers visit Alaska every summer and have a great time of it. Yet there are always some problems and occasionally serious injury or loss of life. Proper gear, time, experience, and prudence should be at the top of the list of things to bring with you to Alaska.

Bears are not your major concern when kayaking in Southeast Alaska. Hypothermia and drowning, which often go together, are the two biggest dangers you face. Either can be caused or exacerbated by paddling in conditions that are beyond your level of skill, which often results from trying to meet an unrealistic schedule.

Time is your most important commodity. Have enough time when kayaking so that you are not tempted to do something of questionable safety because you are trying to meet a schedule. It is better to be late getting back to town and missing that ferry connection or plane reservation than to head into rough waters that are beyond your ability or the abilities of any one of your paddling companions.

Environmental Factors

HYPOTHERMIA

Hypothermia can occur slowly or rapidly, depending on the conditions. You don't have to fall into the water to become hypothermic. In a kayak or in camp, not wearing sufficient clothing can lead to hypothermia. Unless quickly and properly attended to, a victim of hypothermia eventually becomes comatose and dies. A typical progression of symptoms is shivering, speech difficulty, memory loss, exhaustion, and mental confusion.

The patient needs to be treated as gently as possible and kept horizontal. Remove wet clothing and replace them with a sleeping bag and/or put the victim in a sleeping bag with another stripped person or between two people. As in any medical emergency, if there is no breathing and no pulse, CPR is the first consideration. If there is a pulse but no breathing, it is necessary to give rescue breathing.

TIDES & CURRENTS

Tides and currents can be friends or foes. Tides in Southeast Alaska may be bigger and stronger than anything you are used to and can generate remarkable currents. A tide range of 20 feet is not unusual, and maximum spring tides can be as much as 25 feet. Always carry a tide table with you. Every sporting goods store and fishermen's supply house in Alaska hands out free tide tables.

In most places daily tidal currents are not difficult to deal with but can affect point-to-point progress. In Alaska you soon learn to use the tide to your advantage. Arranging to arrive at and depart from a campsite at high tide is not always possible. On a shingle beach arrival or departure on a low tide is not much of an inconvenience, but having to slog across a soft, muddy tidal flat or negotiate slippery algae-covered rocks is difficult and dangerous.

An irritation that can have serious consequences is being routed out of your tent in the middle of the night by a high tide. If you are fortunate, this will only be an inconvenience that generates some funny stories to tell next winter. However, there are campers who misjudged the tide and lost their kayaks; had their food, clothing, and sleeping bags saturated; and ended up having to deal with hypothermia.

Check the tide table every time you camp, and get in the habit of stashing your kayak at least as high as you are camped. *Always* tie it to a tree or big rock and store the paddles inside the boat.

There are some passes in Southeast Alaska that can only be negotiated on slack high or low tide. In deep water use a slack that precedes a current flowing in the direction that you are going.

Salt chucks occur throughout Southeast Alaska. They are formed where lakes or ponds are connected to marine waters by narrow channels and are affected by tidal fluctuations. Flood and ebb currents

Kayaking Southeast Alaska

in these channels produce impressive rapids and overfalls. They are usually negotiable by kayak on high slack water by experienced paddlers. The times at which they flood and ebb may be out of sync with surrounding areas, and it is necessary to watch and wait for the right moment to pass through.

WIND

Rather than trying to remember wind speeds and rules of thumb, my policy is based on whitecaps. If they exist, I don't launch, and if they develop when I am paddling, I head for shore, haul out, and wait for conditions to improve.

Each time you head out on the water consider the relationship of wind to tide. If they are both going the same way you are, it may be great, but things can change fast: Wind and tide in opposition makes for dangerous conditions.

GLACIERS

It is exciting to approach a tidewater glacier in a kayak. Just don't approach too close. The rule of thumb is no closer than 0.5 mile. There are two concerns here. Obviously if you are too close, a calving chunk could fall on you. Ouch! Another problem is that large waves are produced when huge pieces hit the water. If you are too close to the splash, there may not be enough time to turn your boat into the wave crest, and you could capsize.

Stay clear of bergs or any large piece of floating ice. They are constantly melting, and every now and then become unbalanced and suddenly flip over. If you are in the way of the ice or the wave, it can mean big trouble.

TSUNAMIS

Alaska is a high-risk earthquake zone, and I pay attention to potential tsunami events. If I ever "feel" an earthquake when I am camping or kayaking, I head for high ground as quickly as possible (at least 100 feet above sea level) and wait for thirty minutes.

Human Factors

BOAT WAKES

Boat wakes can be especially dangerous in restricted channels, but

they should be a concern everywhere. Even in large sounds and bays, a ship that passed you at some distance away as much as twenty or thirty minutes ago may deliver a dangerous wave to where you are paddling or camping.

The wakes of large ships can be misleading. When you are paddling and the wakes go by, you may hardly notice them because of their low amplitude. But because of their length and number, wake-generated waves tend to pile and come crashing onto shore; they can be extremely hazardous to anyone boarding, exiting, loading, or unloading a kayak.

Plants & Animals

P L A N T S

Most Southeast Alaska plants are either beneficial or benign to humans. There are some good books that will help you identify the plants that you will encounter in Alaska (see Appendix 4). Two plants are important to recognize and avoid: Devils club is a spiny shrub that makes up much of the understory along some parts of the shore. Its broad leaf and stem are spine covered and painful to encounter.

Learn to identify baneberry. Reportedly eating just a few of these berries can bring your trip and your life to an abrupt end. The berries are quite distinctive and can be identified by the shiny, smooth skin that is commonly red but can be white. Baneberry leaves, stems, and roots are poisonous as well.

ANIMALS

Flying insects may not be in your lexicon under potential hazards, but they are in mine. Only the devil however could have invented no-see-ums and white sox, which can be the scourge of the sea kayaker.

No-see-ums are biting gnats and often appear when there is no breeze—early in the morning and in the evening. They usually arrive in huge groups. The only defenses are (a) to cover up totally, including wearing a fine-mesh net over head and face; (b) get in the tent; or (c) paddle away and make your own breeze. Trying to cook or eat in the presence of no-see-ums is hopeless. They get in your nose, mouth, eyes, and ears. Gnat bites sting and last for days.

White sox is another biting, flying insect. They can arrive in a huge delegation or just show up as a small research and study group. They go for any exposed skin, and failing that they try to find a way inside your clothing. The bite lasts for days and can become infected. As with no-see-ums the best protection is to keep covered up.

Deerflies can be obnoxious on sunny, light-air days. However they are slow flying and can be swatted away without much effort. Mosquitos have had a lot of bad press in Alaska, but they live mostly in the interior. I have never had a problem with them in Southeast Alaska.

Paralytic shellfish poisoning (PSP) is caused by eating shellfish that have fed on the marine dinoflagellate *Gonyaulax catanella*. The most famous case occurred two centuries ago near Sitka when about one hundred Aleut hunters of the Russian Baranoff expedition died from eating mussels. Much more recently there have been numerous bivalve poisonings in Southeast Alaska. There is no known antidote or simple field test for PSP, and most cases involve cooked clams and mussels.

After eating contaminated shellfish, the victim experiences a

Kayaking Southeast Alaska

tingling sensation or burning of the lips, gums, or tongue. Numbness and tingling extend to the face, and then neck, fingers, and toes. Other symptoms may include dry mouth, nausea, vomiting, shortness of breath, lack of coordination, a choking sensation, and confused or slurred speech. The most important action is to induce vomiting and get the victim to a medical facility as quickly as possible. However you may not be able to get medical aid when kayaking. Best advice? Don't eat any shellfish when kayaking in Southeast Alaska.

Whales are just about everywhere, but they can be dangerous if you get too close. When you see whales, take note of what they are doing and where they are headed. They are probably either feeding or looking for food and may surface in unpredictable locations.

If the whales you are watching have not surfaced for a longer than what you have observed as an average time, make some noise by tapping your hull if it is a hardshell or shuffling your feet back and forth in a folding kayak. The fact that you don't know where they are may also mean they don't know where you are; making some noise can alert the whales to your presence.

Sea lions will sometimes aggressively approach a kayak. This is probably territorial behavior and can be rather unnerving. If it happens to you, just keep paddling calmly along and don't antagonize the animals. In my experience your visitor will depart if you move into shallow water.

Bears are everyone's concern in Alaska—and with good reason. They are everywhere, they are impressive animals, and under certain circumstances they are dangerous. Avoid getting into those dangerous circumstances. This is not difficult to do even though as an Alaska kayaker, you are always in bear territory.

In Alaska you will be bombarded with bear advice, and much of it is too abbreviated, foolishly simplistic, or designed to be scary. Anyone planning to camp in Alaska has an obligation to themselves and to the bears to learn how to peacefully coexist with these magnificent animals. There are several "bear books" available. I think the best is *Backcountry Bear Basics* by Dave Smith (see Appendix 4). Anyone planning to kayak in Alaska should read this concise, no-nonsense book.

Once you arrive in Alaska, inquire about the local bear situation before you begin a trip. There are Forest Service offices throughout Southeast Alaska, and they welcome your questions. Seasonal feeding activity by bears can be intense in specific areas, and the rangers can advise you of places to avoid. At Glacier Bay the orientation for kayak-camping will include the latest bear advice updates.

Remember that bears are not looking for humans. Quite the contrary. But they are *always* in search of food. Bears find food primarily by their sense of smell. So if your food is well packaged and suspended, there is little chance of its being disturbed. In areas where there are no trees, packaging becomes especially important. In these areas it is also advisable to bury food below rocks to get it out of sight. Consider too using bear-resistant storage containers. The most dangerous bears are those that have found garbage or camp food to eat and therefore associate food with humans.

If you hope to avoid camping any place that you see bear scat, it will be pretty tough to find a campsite. There are a lot of bears in Alaska, and they are constantly roaming around in search of food. Their calling cards are just part of the scene. If the scat is associated with a bear trail, move well away from that path before pitching your tent. If the scat is still steaming . . . be *really* careful!

SOME FUNDAMENTAL BEAR AVOIDANCE CONSIDERATIONS

Select campsites away from bear trails.

Cook and eat away from your tent and in the intertidal zone.

Never have any kind of food in your tent—and that includes snacks.

Hang your food at least 10 feet above the ground and suspend it either between trees or out on a limb.

When hiking, make noise and be especially cautious when rounding blind corners and when near streams and waterfalls: the sound of the water may mask the noise you make.

Read *Backcountry Bear Basics* by Dave Smith.

Being Environmentally Responsible

Low-Impact Kayaking

The National Ocean Survey (NOS) and other organizations recommend getting no closer than 100 yards—a football field's length—to terrestrial and marine mammals. For animals already in the water, 100 yards is usually sufficient. But for marine mammals that are hauled out on the land (seals and sea lions), 100 yards is not enough. In this case another NOS recommendation is relevant. "If your presence causes the animals to alter their behavior, you are too close." Altering behavior means the animals start looking around, begin vocalizing, or begin moving about. You can almost always recognize the beginnings of this nervous behavior.

Kayaking is an excellent way to see bears, and often you can sit quietly in your boat for long periods of time and observe them feeding without being noticed and without disturbing their space. But if the bear is obviously nervous or looks frequently in your direction, you are too close. This could be dangerous to you, and it is definitely bad for the bear.

Watching whales ranks pretty near the top of the list of things sea kayakers like to do in Alaska. You will be amazed at how easy it is to get close to humpbacks, grays, and orcas, but give them space and use discretion and your binoculars when around these impressive animals—for their sake and yours.

When watching whales from your kayak, 100 yards is definitely close enough no matter how tempting it may be to move in closer. In Glacier Bay, the Park Service enforces a quarter-mile rule. If this seems too far away, take heart, there are places, such as Point Adolphus, where whales come in so close to shore that you can simply sit on the beach for a ringside seat.

Low-Impact Camping

In Alaska the significance of environmentally responsible camping and the ramifications of ignoring it are profound. Here the soil is scarce to nonexistent. In most places what you are walking or camping on is in fact a root mat. A campfire built on this surface causes immediate and long-term irreparable damage. Don't do it!

In high latitudes discarded food and human waste break down very slowly. In Southeast Alaska the accepted practice is to deposit body waste as low in the intertidal zone as possible and then to burn toilet paper. The waste material will be broken down and dispersed within the next tidal cycle.

Food left out or improperly stored will invariably attract bears. There are three reasons why this should be avoided: (a) When bears become dependent on human food, they become a "nuisance" and are eventually killed to protect people; (b) Bears and other animals will often ingest some or all of the container—usually plastic—along with the food and become sick; (c) When bears learn to associate free food with people, it puts subsequent campers and kayakers in danger.

Throughout this book I have avoided recommending specific campsites in wilderness areas. This is in line with the policy of the National Park Service and the National Forest Service, and I agree with it. Once tent sites are recommended, they tend to get used repeatedly and soon become "hammered." Fragile, high-latitude rain forest environments just cannot survive repeated use. In most places in Southeast Alaska, there are plenty of places to pitch a tent, and it is seldom necessary to repeatedly occupy the same site. There is as well the unfortunate fact that no matter how careful we are, campsites that are repeatedly used will attract bears, eventually having disastrous consequences for bears and campers.

CAMPSITE CARE

In the simplest of terms, pick your camping place carefully and avoid previously used sites. Avoid destroying or injuring trees. If you want a campfire, build it in the intertidal zone and be sure it is dead out when you are finished. Cook and eat in the intertidal zone. Hang food whenever possible. Any leftover food should be gotten rid of in the water rather than on land. Solid human waste should be deposited as low in the intertidal zone as possible; toilet paper should be burned.

Ketchikan & Vicinity

Ketchikan (population 14,230) is a great kayaking town and the push-off point for a variety of paddling adventures. Everything from half-day guided sightseeing kayak tours of the Ketchikan waterfront and convenient day or longer trips near the southern part of Revillagigedo Island to the popular kayak-camping in Misty Fjords National Monument is available here. More hard-core adventurers will go for the spectacular Behm Canal trip. Ketchikan has frequent ferry service and a variety of flights by Alaska Airlines. The city offers excellent provisioning and outfitting, kayak rentals, and kayak shuttle service. Hotels, B&Bs, and restaurants are plentiful. There is a youth hostel and four campgrounds. Hot showers and laundromats are also readily available.

An impressive new U.S. Forest Service Southeast Alaska Visitor's Center located downtown is well worth a visit. Up-to-the-minute kayaking advice is available from experienced kayak rangers at the Forest Service Ketchikan Ranger District Office at 3031 Tongass Avenue (907–225–2140).

Route 1:

Tongass Narrows

Tongass Narrows is Ketchikan's "main street." This channel is used by cruise ships, commercial tugs, fishing boats, and floatplanes. Guided kayak trips operate on the Narrows from downtown Ketchikan, and there are some good places here to launch for cruising the waterfront; crossing the Narrows to Pennock Island, Black Sand Beach, and Gravina Island; or heading up to Totum Bight.

TRIP HIGHLIGHTS: Kayaking in Tongass Narrows is not exactly a wilderness experience, but it is of cultural interest. However, across the Narrows there are scenic spots, and in minutes you can quickly "get away from it all."

TRIP RATING:
Beginner: OK for beginners if accompanied by an experienced paddler. Crossing the currents in the Narrows requires some skill and the opportunity to develop skills in ferrying.

TRIP DURATION: In and around town is an easy three- to four-hour paddle. Plan five hours to go the 7 miles around Pennock Island. If you add on Black Sand Beach, make it a full day or plan to camp there. A round-trip to Totem Bight is 13 miles; day trip.

NAVIGATION AIDS: NOAA chart 17428.

TIDAL INFORMATION: Use the tides to help you along your way; always factor them in when crossing the Narrows. Free tide tables are available at any marine supply store.

CAUTIONS: Busy harbor traffic and currents when crossing Tongass Narrows require attention.

TRIP PLANNING: Early morning is the most peaceful time to be paddling in or across the Narrows, but anytime is OK with caution. From 4:00 to 8:00 A.M. is excellent in the summer.

LAUNCH SITE: The two municipal marinas, Bar Point Basin and Thomas Basin, are easy and convenient launch areas. There is a limited amount of free twenty-four- and seventy-two-hour parking at Bar Point Basin. With a bit of effort, you can also launch at the ferry terminal.

DIRECTIONS

HARBOR TRIP: Ketchikan is spread out for 4.0 miles along the water, so head north or south depending on where you put in. You can paddle into **Thomas Basin** and then up Ketchikan Creek at high water and watch all of the tourists from the boardwalk above watching you watching them. Southeast along the Narrows you will pass fish processing plants, boat repair facilities, and the Coast Guard station. Continue on as far as the suburb of **Saxman** about 2.5 miles southeast from Thomas Basin boat harbor.

PENNOCK ISLAND: The island lies directly across **Tongass Narrows** from

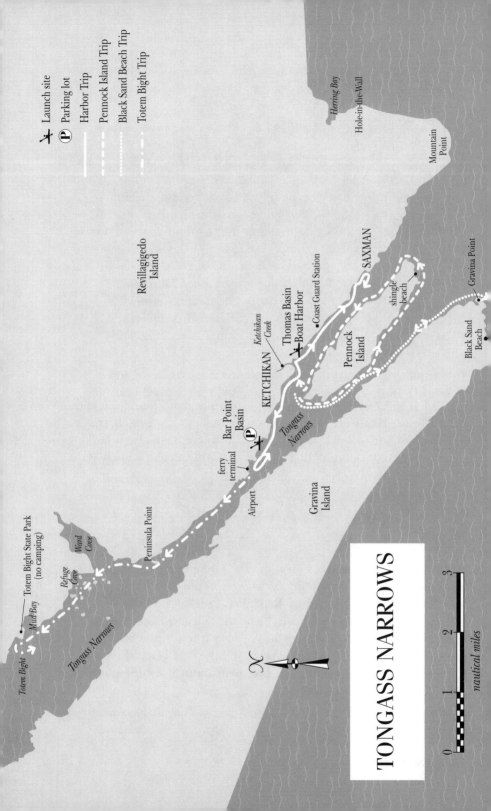

TONGASS NARROWS

Launch site
Parking lot
Harbor Trip
Pennock Island Trip
Black Sand Beach Trip
Totem Bight Trip

Revillagigedo Island

Totem Bight State Park (no camping)
Totem Bight
Mud Bay
Ward Cove
Refuge Cove
Tongass Narrows
Peninsula Point

Airport
ferry terminal
Bar Point Basin
P
KETCHIKAN
Ketchikan Creek
Thomas Basin
Boat Harbor
Coast Guard Station
SAXMAN
Tongass Narrows

Gravina Island

Pennock Island
shingle beach
Black Sand Beach
Gravina Point

Mountain Point
Hole-in-the-Wall
Herring Bay

nautical miles
0   1   2   3

downtown Ketchikan. There is a small shingle beach on the southwest corner that makes a nice picnic stop. The back (west) side is so remote and peaceful that you will wonder what happened to the frantic pace of Ketchikan.

BLACK SAND BEACH: This destination can be an extension of the Pennock Island trip; combined they make for a full day of paddling or paddling/camping. **Black Sand Beach** is in a small bight west of **Gravina Point** on **Gravina Island**, about 2.0 miles southwest of Pennock Island. The water here is crystal clear and lots of sea stars and anemones decorate the surface below you. There is a state-maintained shelter at the head of the bay. *Caution:* This bay is fully exposed to the southwest. Keep a weather eye out for an increase in wind from that direction. If southwest winds begin, it is best to skedaddle out of there and head for the channel on one or the other side of Pennock Island.

The way to Black Sand Beach can also be the beginning of a circumnavigation of Gravina Island. The island circumference is about 60 miles, and if you are considering this trip, budget at least five days. This trip is for experienced kayakers only.

TOTEM BIGHT: Use the tide to help paddle the 6–7 miles to Totem Bight from Bar Point or Thomas Basin. The route takes you past the ferry docks on the north end of town, across **Ward Cove**, and around some scenic small islands. Slip across the narrow entrance to **Refuge Cove**, just as you cross **Mud Bay**, you will see a group of totem poles in the state park. Round the point into the next small bay. Here you can haul out while visiting the park. Carry your boat well above the water and tie or anchor it. After visiting the free park, return to Ketchikan the way you came.

Route 2:

━━ ━ ━━ ━ ━ ━ ━━ ━━ ━ ━━ ━ ━━ ━━ ━ ━ ━━ ━━ ━━ ➤

George Inlet

George Inlet lies a few miles southeast of Ketchikan and is easily accessible from town by road. Much of the time George Inlet offers protected waters for kayaking—especially in its upper reaches.

TRIP HIGHLIGHTS: Scenic paddling, waterfowl, wilderness camping, marine and terrestrial mammals.

TRIP RATING:

Beginner: Kayakers with only a little experience will have no problems here if they are willing to stay off the water when the wind picks up. Ability to camp in remote locations is important.

TRIP DURATION: From Hole-in-the-Wall marina to the head of George Inlet is 17 miles. Plan to camp at least two nights.

NAVIGATION AIDS: NOAA chart 17428.

TIDAL INFORMATION: George Inlet tides are not difficult. However to make your trip easier, plan passages with tide flow in your favor.

CAUTIONS: Salt Lagoon at the head of George Inlet is a salt chuck with dangerous rapids. Even very experienced paddlers only attempt this on high slack water.

TRIP PLANNING: Consult the tide table to assist in paddling and for selecting campsites. Obtain an extended weather forecast before setting out.

LAUNCH SITES: Hole-in-the-Wall marina (7.6 miles from downtown). Free use for launching and free day parking. It is necessary to carry boat and gear down a fairly steep ramp. Mountain Point boat harbor is closer to town (5.6 miles), easier to use, but less convenient for George Inlet.

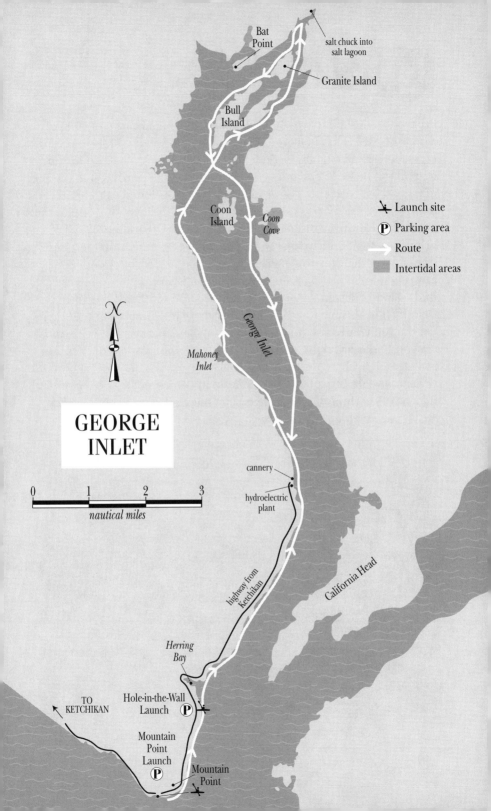

Launch site

ⓟ Parking area

→ Route

Intertidal areas

Bat
Point

salt chuck into
salt lagoon

Granite Island

Bull
Island

Coon
Island

*Coon
Cove*

George Inlet

N

*Mahoney
Inlet*

GEORGE
INLET

0   1   2   3
nautical miles

cannery

hydroelectric
plant

highway from Ketchikan

California Head

*Herring
Bay*

TO
KETCHIKAN

Hole-in-the-Wall
Launch   ⓟ

Mountain
Point
Launch
ⓟ

Mountain
Point

Proceed from the **Hole-in-the-Wall** launch site on a northeast course along the west side of George Inlet. At 1.0 mile beyond Hole-in-the-Wall cross **Herring Bay**. Then begin a 3.5-mile stretch with little opportunity to haul out or stop. The inlet curves around to the northwest at the site of a small **hydroelectric power plant** and an abandoned **cannery**. If there is any wind this day, you can expect it to either improve or worsen at this point. You can stop here temporarily if necessary. Another 4.0 miles brings you to **Mahoney Inlet** with some impressive waterfalls and nice camping on the north side. From here on are numerous good campsites, including **Coon Island**, the small islands near Coon Cove, **Bull Island**, and some very small islands on the southeast side of Bull Island. (It is possible to camp most anywhere in Upper George Inlet.) On the return trip you may want to favor the eastern side if wind and sea conditions are right, crossing to the west when the cannery comes in sight.

Seals are present and occasionally orcas come here to feed. Now and then a solitary humpback whale cruises these waters. Watch for black bears grazing along the shore.

Route 3:

▬ ▬ ▬ ▬ ▬ ▬ ▬ ▬ ▬ ▬ ▬ ▬ ▬ ▬ ▬ ➤

Clover Passage & Naha Bay

Clover Passage, 15 miles northwest of Ketchikan, is a nice area for a variety of day trips or longer kayak-camping excursions. Even on breezy days you can usually find protected water in the lee of the numerous islands within the Passage. Marbled murrelets, scoters, and in late spring, Barrow's goldeneyes are found here in great abundance. I have seen black bears along the shore, and eagles and ravens are always present. Harbor seals typically haul out on the rocky islets behind Hump and Betton Islands. Naha Bay at the northeast end of Clover Passage contains the old cannery town of Loring and scenic Roosevelt Lagoon with its well-maintained hiking trails.

TRIP HIGHLIGHTS: Protected paddling in most wind conditions, birding, beach combing, campground or wilderness camping, and hiking trails.

TRIP RATING:
Beginner/Intermediate: Basic skills are needed for day trips or longer, but even beginners if accompanied by more experienced paddlers will find this a convenient locale for developing skills.

TRIP DURATION: From Knudson Cove or Settlers Cove, paddlers can make jaunts of just a few hours and miles, day-long excursions of 8 or 10 miles, or kayak-camping trips. The longest trip is to Roosevelt Lagoon—nearly 24 miles round-trip.

NAVIGATION AIDS: NOAA chart 17422.

TIDAL INFORMATION: Tide range here can exceed 20 feet, but in the summer it is typically between 15 and 17 feet. Tidal currents are not difficult or dangerous except for the salt chuck at Roosevelt Lagoon.

CAUTIONS: Numerous sports fishing and small excursion boats use Clover Passage, but paddling near shore will keep you away from this traffic. The entrance to Roosevelt Lagoon is a tidal salt chuck with rapids flowing in or out most of the time. This should only be attempted by experienced kayakers. If you want to enter the lagoon, it is easier to portage across the old tramway nearby. The tramway car no longer exists, but the tramway surface is negotiable.

TRIP PLANNING: Get a weather update and check the tide table before setting off. For day trips there are plenty of alternatives if the wind shifts. Be flexible.

LAUNCH SITE: At Knudson Cove (14.5 miles from Ketchikan) you can launch for free from a floating dock. There is free day parking or seventy-two-hour fee parking. Five miles north of Knudson Cove is Settlers Cove Campground where there is no charge for day use, and you can launch from the beach. The easiest access to the beach is at campsite 14.

DIRECTIONS

For day trips or even overnighters out of **Knudson Cove** and **Settlers Cove**, let the tide, the wind, and what you feel up for be your guides. If you are a bit short on experience, start out with some easy jaunts along the shore.

With light winds and favorable tides, consider crossing to the islands along the northwest side of **Clover Passage. Hump**, **Back**, **Joe**, **Grant**, **Stack**, **Moser**, and **Cedar Islands** all make for nice circumnavigations. The southwest corner of Grant Island has a shingle beach, and a slender peninsula on the southeast corner of Back Island offers a small but charming site for camping. Betton Island is an excellent choice for a circumnavigation in good weather, offering pleasant paddling among the **Tatoosh Islands.** *Sidetrips:* At the north end of Clover Passage, Moser Bay and Long Arm are worth exploring. They can also be convenient hideouts if the wind kicks up for a while. *Farther along:* In Naha Bay are the remains of the town of Loring, once the site of a major cannery. In its hay day in the 1800s, Loring was bigger and more important than Ketchikan, and steamers from San Francisco and Seattle came here. Today it is mostly a weekend retreat, but there is a state dock that you can tie up to for free. There are no stores or services.

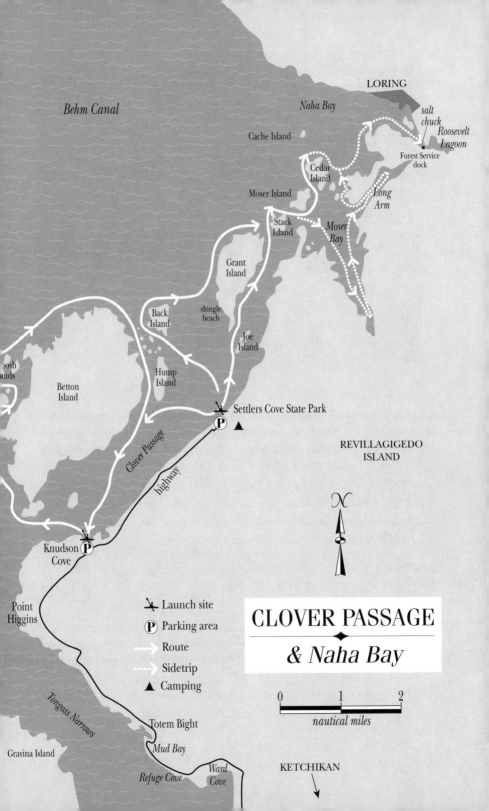

LORING

Behm Canal

Naha Bay

salt chuck

Cache Island

Roosevelt Lagoon

Cedar Island

Forest Service dock

Moser Island

Long Arm

Stack Island

Moser Bay

Grant Island

Back Island

shingle beach

Joe Island

Hump Island

Betton Island

bosh nds

Settlers Cove State Park

Clover Passage

REVILLAGIGEDO ISLAND

highway

N

Knudson Cove

Point Higgins

⚲ Launch site

Ⓟ Parking area

→ Route

⇢ Sidetrip

▲ Camping

CLOVER PASSAGE
& Naha Bay

0   1   2

nautical miles

Tongass Narrows

Gravina Island

Totem Bight

Mud Bay

Refuge Cove

Ward Cove

KETCHIKAN

At the head of Naha Bay, you can paddle to a Forest Service dock near the entrance to Roosevelt Lagoon. Even if you don't kayak in the lagoon, a 2.5-mile forest trail leads around the north side and then continues 2.0 more miles on to Jordan Lake. An additional 2.0 miles of trail goes to Heckman Lake. There are Forest Service cabins at Jordan and Heckman Lakes.

Where to Stay

CAMPING   Settlers Cove State Park has campsites for tents and RVs. Rest rooms and fresh water are available. This is an excellent place to stay while making day trips or as a starting and ending place for the longer trips. When paddling elsewhere, you can camp anywhere on Forest Service land. Also, from the entrance to Roosevelt Lagoon there are trails leading to USFS cabins at Jordan Lake and Heckman Lake. For either of these cabins reservations are necessary; a use fee must be paid in advance. (Appendix 2 describes the procedure.)

Route 4:

━━ ━━ ━━ ━━ ━━ ━━ ━━ ━━ ━━ ━━ ━━ ━━ ━━ ➤

Misty Fjords National Monument

This beautiful area is still one of Alaska's secrets. The most famous—and therefore most popular—places within Misty Fjords National Monument are Rudyerd Bay and Walker Cove. But don't overlook the rest of the area. There is a lot of scenic grandeur in other inlets and bays that few of Misty's visitors ever find. Most of Misty Fjords is remote and wild country, a haven for ducks, brown and black bear, Sitka deer, mink, river otters, and in a few places, moose. Humpbacks and orcas, porpoise, sea lions, and seals ply the waters of Behm Canal and the inlets. The steep and sometimes sheer fjord walls are keys to the area's scenic allure, but they also make camping sites hard to come by.

It is possible to reach Misty Fjords by paddling to and/or from Ketchikan. However the round-trip distance to Walker or Rudyerd is more than 40 miles, and paddling will add at least two days on each end of your trip. Many kayakers therefore choose to use one of the delivery and pickup services from Ketchikan.

TRIP HIGHLIGHTS: Magnificent steep fjord walls, old-growth rain forest, wilderness camping, birding, and viewing of marine and terrestrial animals.

TRIP RATING:

Beginner: Those who get dropped off in one of the bays, inlets, or coves and restrict their paddling to that local area will typically find calm conditions that allow beginner level skills.

Advanced: Those who paddle all the way to and from Ketchikan to Misty Fjords need to be experienced paddlers with plenty of time. In every group however there should be at least one person who is knowledgeable in wilderness camping.

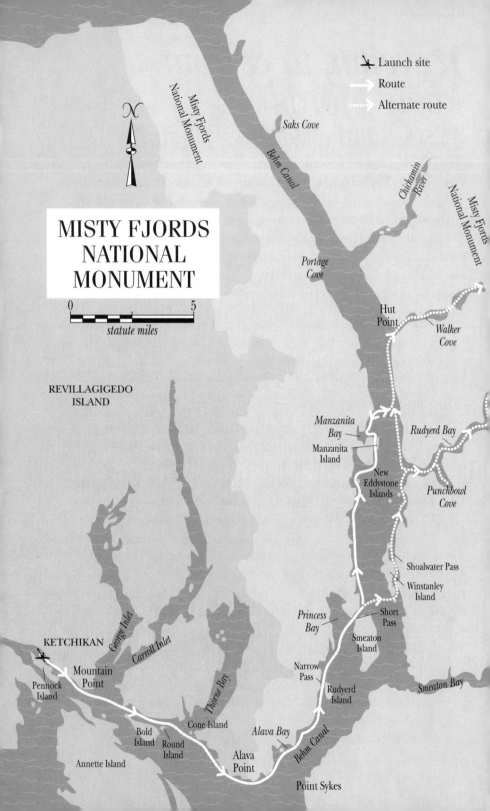

Traveling to & from Misty Fjords

If you decide to use a delivery and pickup service for your visit to Misty Fjords, there are some choices. Alaska Cruises makes a run every day to Misty Fjords in its high-speed catamaran and does drop-offs and pickups at their floating dock at the head of Rudyerd Bay. Silver King Charters, Alaska Aquamarine Experience, and Southeast Sea Kayaks can all arrange kayak transportation at a variety of locations in Misty Fjords. This service is more to the liking of most sea kayakers because it means you can spend less time in busy Rudyerd Inlet or even avoid it altogether, and you can paddle from one place to another without repeating any part of the trip.

TRIP DURATION: Plan on spending at least four to six days in Misty Fjords. Those who paddle one or both ways from or to Ketchikan are looking at easily 120 miles of paddling. Inside the monument you can paddle as much or as little as you wish. However from a drop-off in Rudyerd Bay to Walker Cove and Manzanita Bay, then back to Rudyerd is 60 miles.

NAVIGATION AIDS: NOAA chart 17424 is a highly detailed chart with more detail than is necessary. More realistic options are the USGS topo map *Ketchikan* (1:250,000), or better yet NOAA chart 17420. Nearly as good and less expensive is the U.S. Forest Service map, *Misty Fjords Monument Map* (see Appendix 3). The last however is printed on paper that has a short life.

TIDAL INFORMATION: Consult tide tables for paddling and camping. Ranges are typical for the rest of the Ketchikan area, and currents are easily manageable—with the exception of the Alava Point area (discussed later). Plan daily paddling to take advantage of tide.

CAUTIONS: There is abundant boat traffic in Rudyerd Bay, which creates significant wakes for paddlers to move through. Wakes are especially dangerous when loading and unloading kayaks on the beach. Sea conditions can be rough at times within Behm Canal, especially in the vicinity of Alava Bay and Alava Point, which is exposed to the southwest ocean swells and winds.

TRIP PLANNING: Talk to Forest Service personnel at the district ranger station in Ketchikan before paddling in Misty Fjords. If kayaking out and back from Ketchikan, take along a VHF handheld radio that can also pick up weather broadcasts. Get an extended weather forecast before setting out.

LAUNCH SITE: When leaving from Ketchikan any of the small boat harbors are convenient. If you are getting hauled in, your starting point can be either the floating dock at the head of Rudyerd Bay or with some transporters almost any point of your choice. Popular options are Manzanita Bay, Hut Point at the entrance to Walker Cove, and Winstanley Island.

DIRECTIONS

If you leave from Ketchikan, follow the shoreline southeast to **Mountain Point**, cross **George Inlet**, and continue along to the north of **Bold** and **Round Islands** past **Cone Island**, and eventually round into **Behm Canal** heading northeast at **Alava Point**.

In Behm Canal continue on through **Narrow Pass** and **Short Pass** and perhaps on to **Manzanita Bay**—an excellent camping spot. Or in favorable conditions consider crossing the canal at Short Pass, then heading north to **Winstanley Island** and **Shoalwater Pass** on the way to **Rudyerd Bay** or **Walker Cove**.

Where to Stay & Where to Hike

CAMPING Camping is permitted anywhere in Misty Fjords National Monument. However opportunities are limited by topography and sometimes by bear density. Check with Forest Service rangers for current conditions. Also, there are a number of Forest Service cabins in Misty Fjords that you can reserve and pay for in advance (see Appendix 2). **HIKING** There are some excellent short hiking trails in Misty Fjords. Ask the Forest Service folks in Ketchikan for the Recreation Opportunity Guides (ROGs) for the trails in Misty.

Route 5:

▬ ▬ ▬ ▬ ▬ ▬ ▬ ▬ ▬ ▬ ▬ ▬ ▬ ▬ ▬ ➡

Behm Canal (Revillagigedo Island Circumnavigation)

Behm Canal is the ultimate Ketchikan Area trip. The canal is a natural waterway that surrounds the west, north, and east sides of Revillagigedo Island and includes some of the trips so far described plus many more. It is a trip of between 120 and 150 miles depending on launch and haul-out points. It could probably be done in ten days, but I don't consider it worth doing unless you have three weeks to really enjoy the adventure and take time to explore at least a few of the many bays and inlets along the way. Sidetrips can add as many as 100 miles.

TRIP HIGHLIGHTS: Beautiful scenery, hot springs, bears, waterfowl, marine mammals, berry picking, wilderness camping, Misty Fjords, solitude, old-growth forest.

TRIP RATING:

Beginner/Intermediate: Basic kayaking skills are sufficient for most of the trip, but unpredictable or unexpected weather can tax even experienced paddlers. Best advice for a beginner, especially, is to have someone along who is experienced. Difficulties can be mitigated significantly by getting off or staying off the water when conditions become unfavorable. The decision to do this is essential, whether it is based on experience or on common sense. One thing is certain: A Behm Canal trip is an opportunity to develop experience under a variety of paddling conditions.

TRIP DURATION: Anything less than ten days will be sort of a marathon effort. The minimum distance is only about 150 miles, but it will be unusual to not lose at least one day per week to weather that precludes paddling.

NAVIGATION AIDS: NOAA chart 17420.

TIDAL INFORMATION: Each day's run should be made to work with the tides. The west entrance to Blind Pass at the top of Behm Canal goes dry at low tide.

CAUTIONS: Use care when paddling the long stretches of Behm Canal on windy days. There can be a pretty good fetch in a lot of the area. Having to deal with strong southwest winds in the vicinity of Alava Point is no picnic. Also at Alava Point even under favorable wind conditions, opposing currents are challenging.

TRIP PLANNING: Talk with Forest Service kayakers at the district ranger office in Ketchikan just before beginning trip for any recommendations or information they may care to offer.

LAUNCH SITE: An excellent starting place is Settlers Cove State Park on Clover Passage west of Ketchikan. Or use other starting points mentioned for Ketchikan trips.

DIRECTIONS

For a complete Behm Canal trip, the usual procedure is to paddle north on the west arm of **Behm Canal** and south on the east arm to take advantage of most favorable typical winds. There is no specific route of travel, and camping is possible anywhere you find a desirable site.

It is possible to begin from one of the downtown boat basins or from the ferry terminal and head northwest in **Tongass Narrows**. Other kayakers with road transportaton may choose to begin their trip from **Knudson Cove** or **Settlers Cove State Park**. Head north in **Clover Passage** and through **Naha Bay**. In nearly every case expect and plan to camp in one of the coves or bays on the east side of Behm Canal. **Traitors Cove**, **Neets Bay**, **Gedney Pass**, and **Klu Bay** all offer fascinating sidetrips.

Near the top of Behm Canal the protected area of **Blind Pass** is a beautiful calm area to visit. Note that the west entrance is negotiable on high water. Near the north end of **Bailey Bay** is the Forest Service trail to the hot spring at Lake Shelocum. There is room to camp near the beginning of the trail, and there is also a lean-to at the hot spring. The paddle up **Bell Arm** and into **Anchor Pass** is usually quiet and peaceful.

Before beginning the trip south down the east arm of Behm Canal and into Misty Fjords National Monument, spend some time exploring

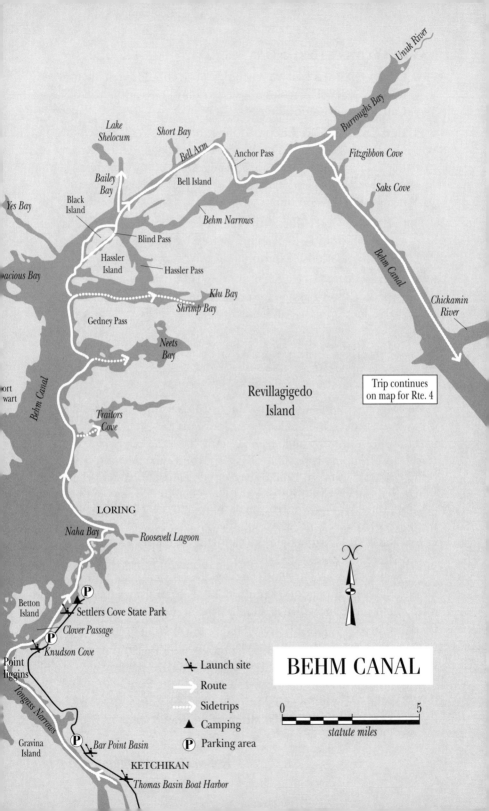

Unuk River

Burroughs Bay

Lake Shelocum

Short Bay

Bell Arm

Anchor Pass

Fitzgibbon Cove

Bailey Bay

Bell Island

Saks Cove

Yes Bay

Black Island

Behm Narrows

Blind Pass

Behm Canal

Hassler Island

Hassler Pass

Klu Bay

...acious Bay

Shrimp Bay

Chickamin River

Gedney Pass

Neets Bay

Trip continues on map for Rte. 4

...ort ...wart

Behm Canal

Traitors Cove

Revillagigedo Island

LORING

Naha Bay

Roosevelt Lagoon

N

Betton Island

⚓ Settlers Cove State Park

P

Clover Passage

P

Knudson Cove

Point ...iggins

Tongass Narrows

⚓ Launch site

→ Route

····> Sidetrips

▲ Camping

P Parking area

BEHM CANAL

0 — 5

statute miles

Gravina Island

P ⚓ Bar Point Basin

KETCHIKAN

⚓ Thomas Basin Boat Harbor

Burroughs Bay and the lower part of the **Unuk River**. When heading south, there is the opportunity to camp in **Fitzgibbon Cove**, **Saks Cove**, and especially **Chickamin River**. Unless the currents are high, it is possible to kayak some distance up the river. (The route between Misty Fjords National Monument and Ketchikan is described in Rte. 4.)

Anywhere in Behm Canal you can expect to see orcas and humpbacks. River otters will be everywhere, and mink and porcupine are often found along the shore. In mid- to late summer this whole area is excellent for salmonberries, blueberries, and red huckleberries. But be prepared to share with the bears. Generally on **Revillagigedo Island** you will see black bears, and on the adjacent mainland, brown bears. But bears are great swimmers so the rule has many exceptions. You can be sure that if you kayak quietly and keep your eyes open, there will be plenty of opportunities to see bears on this trip. Most of the area is prime old-growth forest; nights spent camping on sphagnum moss are memorable.

For those who wish to make an extended trip in Behm Canal, the opportunity exists to make arrangements in advance to be resupplied by a floatplane at a predetermined location.

Where to Stay & Where to Hike

CAMPING The last opportunity for staying in a campground is Settlers Cove State Park. Otherwise you can camp almost any place. In addition, there are a number of Forest Service cabins along Behm Canal that are either at sea level or can be reached by hiking from the water. Cabins are all available on a reservation basis (see Appendix 2). Cabin stays work especially well for first nights if you are being dropped off somewhere when beginning your trip. **HIKING** Throughout Behm Canal there are a number of short hiking trails that begin at sea level and often take you to a scenic lake. The Forest Service in Ketchikan can supply you with a Recreational Opportunity Guide (ROG) for each of their trails.

Petersburg & Vicinity

Petersburg (population 3,400) is the consummate no nonsense Alaska fishing town. Fish processing is what the town does best. Your initial impression will be of a busy harbor with fishing boats off-loading their catches, while crews repair their gear and get ready to head out for the next opening. This may leave you wondering what Petersburg has to do with kayaking. What is going on in Petersburg is less important to the kayaker than its role as the gateway to nearby spectacular paddling.

The Stikine River and Stikine Delta, Le Conte Bay and Le Conte Glacier, Wrangell Narrows, and the route through Rocky Pass to Kake are all accessed from Petersburg. Each of these offers a different kind of kayaking adventure and an exciting challenge to adventuresome paddlers.

Petersburg is a stop on the Alaska Marine Highway ferry system to and from Bellingham, Washington, as well as a connecting point to other area towns. A lot of people look forward to the ferry trip to Petersburg if only for the thrill of traveling through Wrangell Narrows. Alaska Airlines makes scheduled stops at Petersburg, and there are a variety of fixed-gear and floatplane services to get you to and from the town. Petersburg has several restaurants, hotels, B&Bs, a laundromat, hot showers, and a campground. Kayaks can be rented in Petersburg, and guided paddling trips originate from here.

Wrangell

The town of Wrangell (population 2,590) is only 42 miles away from Petersburg and is another of the stops on the ferry system. It is also serviced by Alaska Airlines. For those traveling into the Stikine River and Stikine Delta, it is as convenient as Petersburg, and there are boat services in Wrangell that will transport kayaks up the Stikine River. Wrangell is not a significant paddling center however; it lacks kayak guide services, kayak rentals, and other significant support services.

Route 6:

Stikine River & Delta

T he Stikine River area is exciting country that offers a startlingly different kind of kayaking from the rest of Southeast Alaska. Even though the Stikine is a major river, the paddling in its lower reaches is not at all *river kayaking* as the term is understood by aficionados of that pastime. If you go about it right, the Stikine is an easy kind of kayaking that combines great scenery with ample opportunities to see black bear, moose, and beaver. Camping spots are abundant and easy to access, and there is even a hot spring at which the Forest Service maintains a hot tub in a take-your-breath-away setting.

TRIP HIGHLIGHTS: The potential for easy "downhill" paddling. Great scenery and opportunities to view wildlife.

TRIP RATING:

Beginner: Easy for beginners accompanied by experienced friends or qualified guide. Experienced paddlers will have an easy and enjoyable time.

TRIP DURATION: Variable depending on put-in point. From the Canadian border on the Stikine River to the "old boat ramp" on the south end of Mitkof Island is about 30 miles. The minimum time to cover this is four days; but this sojourn could extend enjoyably to ten days or two weeks. You can easily cover 20 miles of river a day on the way downstream, but there are a lot of interesting sidetrips along the way. It pays to reserve one day for getting across the delta. Although the crossing does not take a full day, it may be necessary to camp and wait to have the tide you want.

NAVIGATION AIDS: NOAA chart 17360 shows the marine portions of the area, but has no details of the river. The U.S. Forest Service map *Stikine River—Canoe/Kayak Routes* takes you up to the Canadian border and is easy and convenient to use. Alternatives are the 1:250,000-scale USGS topo maps *Petersburg* and *Bradfield Canal*. For more detail use the 1:63,360-scale USGS *Petersburg* (C-1, C-2) and *Bradfield Canal* (C-6) maps, which also take you up to the Canadian border. For travel into Canada use the following Canada topo maps: at 1:250,000 scale, 104B and 104G; at 1:50,000 scale, 104B/12, B/13, G/4, G/5, G/11, G/12, and G/14. These maps follow the Stikine River to the town of Telegraph Creek about 120 river miles from the Canada–U.S. border. (Appendix 3 tells you how to find and purchase Canadian topographic maps.)

TIDAL INFORMATION: Tides are of no significance until you reach the delta, and there they become the controlling factor. Large parts of the Stikine Delta are difficult to impossible at any time other than high water. Plan accordingly.

CAUTIONS: Anyone paddling on the Stikine must know how to "ferry" across areas of fast-moving water. Much of the river is easy paddling or even drifting. But in a few places it is necessary to cross from one side to the other with very fast water, and a kayaker needs to be confident in her or his skills. If this maneuver is new to you, be sure to take your first Stikine trip with an experienced guide.

There is the possibility of grounding in the delta, which can be

Stikine River & Delta

inconvenient or dangerous in windy conditions. Use discretion when preparing to cross these vast shallow water areas. If in doubt stop and camp until conditions improve.

TRIP PLANNING: If you plan to be in Canada for part of the trip, it is necessary to contact both Canadian and U.S. Customs to let them know the dates on which you will be crossing their borders, even though there are no guards or checkpoints on the river. Positive identification is required, and those who are citizens of countries other than Canada or the United States may need to complete some paperwork.

Purchase a copy of the U.S. Forest Service's *Stikine River— Canoe/Kayak Routes.* It is surely the best guide for descending the river from the Canadian border. It shows several alternative routes along the different river arms, . . . and nearly everyone will consider a stop at the hot tub at Chief Shakes Hot Springs on the Hot Springs Slough route.

LAUNCH SITE: Those "heroes and heroines" who think they want to paddle up the Stikine will probably want to start out from Wrangell, although it is possible to start from Petersburg or from the old boat ramp near the south end of Mitkof Highway on Mitkof Island. In either of those scenarios, it is a matter of getting across the delta.

If wiser heads prevail and you charter a boat or floatplane going up river or go with a guided trip, possibile launch sites are limited only by your time and budget. Some paddlers begin as far up river as the Canadian town of Telegraph Creek, but most select points 50 miles or less up river from the Canadian border. Although well off the beaten track, there is a road to Telegraph Creek.

DIRECTIONS

How you run the Stikine obviously depends on where you put in, the river's stage, and where you plan to end up. The routes shown on the accompanying map are based on those suggested by the Forest Service guidebook. Each group will want to improvise as it goes along the river.

There are some interesting stops and sidetrips to make along the way if you have sufficient time. Those who put in above the Canada– U.S.

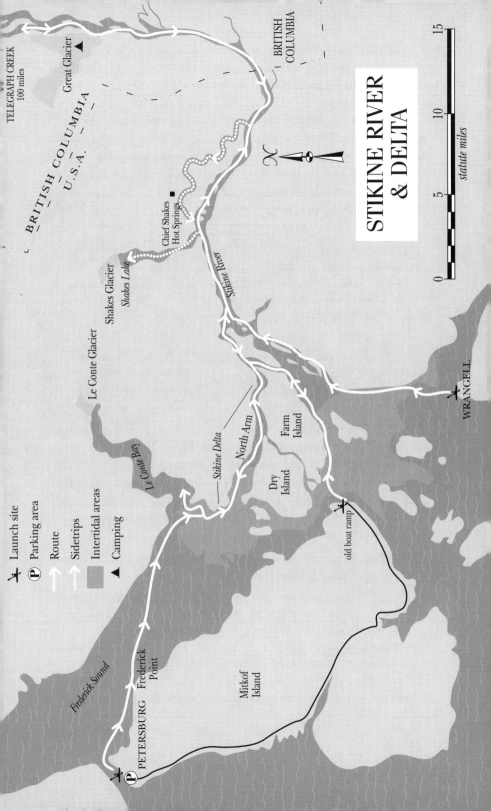

STIKINE RIVER & DELTA

Legend

- ✈ Launch site
- Ⓟ Parking area
- → Route
- ⇨ Sidetrips
- ▨ Intertidal areas
- ▲ Camping

TELEGRAPH CREEK
100 miles

Great Glacier ▲

BRITISH COLUMBIA
U.S.A.

BRITISH COLUMBIA

Shakes Glacier

Le Conte Glacier

Shakes Lake

Chief Shakes
Hot Springs ■

Stikine River

Le Conte Bay

Stikine Delta

North Arm

WRANGELL ✈

Farm Island

Dry Island

old boat ramp ✈

Frederick Sound

Frederick Point

Mitkof Island

PETERSBURG ✈ Ⓟ

statute miles

0   5   10   15

border will want to include a stop at **Great Glacier**, where there is a camping and picnicking area and an enjoyable hiking trail to the glacier. There are a lot of large and small sloughs along the river that are fascinating to explore. They are obvious as you paddle along. Enter them as your daily schedule permits. Downriver from **Chief Shakes Hot Springs** is the popular Shakes Lake route, which takes you the 3.0 miles to **Shakes Lake** and **Shakes Glacier**. (After crossing the Stikine Delta you can tie in with Rte. 7.)

Where to Stay

CAMPING   It is possible to camp anywhere you choose along the river. *Caution:* Always camp and secure kayaks well above river level. The river can rise rapidly and unexpectedly overnight depending on rainfall far upstream. Also, there are five Forest Service cabins along the U.S. part of the Stikine River and seven cabins on the Stikine Delta (see Appendix 2).

Going Up River

The Forest Service sells a very useful guide map of kayak routes for the Stikine River (see Appendix 3). However the clear implication in the text accompanying the map is that you can work your way up the river by following back eddies and now and then "lining" along the bank—and yes some people actually do it that way! Personally after paddling down the Stikine there is no way I would want to try and work my way upstream against the current by paddle and lining. Leave self-propelled upstream travel to spawning salmon!

To really enjoy a Stikine River trip spend the extra money and charter a boat to take you and your kayak upstream. Better yet participate in one of the trips offered by Tongass Kayak Adventures of Petersburg.

Route 7:

▬ ▬ ▬ ▬ ▬ ▬ ▬ ▬ ▬ ▬ ▬ ▬ ▬ ▬ ➤

Le Conte Bay & Glacier

Le Conte is the southernmost tidal glacier in the United States. Though not often mentioned as a major attraction in the literature, it is also one of the most accessible. The setting is beautiful with a magnificent waterfall nearby, a variety of seabirds, and nonstop views of seals lounging on floating ice blocks. In the background are impressive views of glaciated peaks, hanging glaciers, and snowfields.

TRIP HIGHLIGHTS: Scenery, wildlife, and glacier-proximity kayaking.

TRIP RATING:

Beginner/Advanced: Those paddling from Petersburg or the south end of Mitkof Island need to be experienced kayakers or else traveling in company with experienced friends or guides. However if you elect to reach Le Conte Bay by using a kayak delivery service, it is possible for paddlers with relatively little experience to make this trip.

TRIP DURATION: If going from and returning to Mitkof Island this excursion can be done in minimum of three days by strong paddlers with good weather conditions. Those bringing their kayaks to Le Conte by a powerboat can make this a day trip.

NAVIGATION AIDS: NOAA chart 17360 is minimal but sufficient.

TIDAL INFORMATION: As the tide moves so do the large and small blocks of floating ice in the bay. It is necessary to keep this in mind to avoid being boxed in.

CAUTIONS: Avoid approaching within a half mile of the glacier face. Keep a weather eye out for how the berg bits and ice chunks are floating in the bay. A combination of wind and tide can cause them to form an impenetrable wall that could trap you in the floating ice field. Do not approach close to large ice blocks as they can flip over without warning.

TRIP PLANNING: Obtain a current weather forecast and be aware of the times of the tides.

LAUNCH SITE: It is possible to launch from the old boat ramp near the end of the Mitkof Highway on the south end of Mitkof Island. One then has about 12 miles to cover while dealing with the shallow waters of the wide tidal delta. Launching from Petersburg entails the crossing of Frederick Sound. Those who bring their kayaks to Le Conte Bay by powerboat have the option to launch from most anywhere in the bay.

DIRECTIONS

Leaving from **Petersburg**, head southeast to **Frederick Point**. If conditions appear favorable head to the north side of the sound and proceed southeast along shore to Le Conte Bay. Once you round **Indian Point**, there are numerous places to camp, or you can proceed up bay past **Timber Point** (on your right) and on to **Thunder Point** (to the left). Before passing Thunder Point you should choose a campsite because farther on the shoreline becomes more rocky and steep. Round-trip covers about 52 miles.

From the south end of **Mitkof Island**, it is a matter of finding your way across the delta at high tide or skirting it by padding an arc from the vicinity of **Cosmos Point** around to **Indian Point** and then proceeding as just discussed. Return trips are the reverse. A round-trip of 56 miles—about the same as traveling from Petersburg.

Once in upper Le Conte Bay, it is a matter of cautiously making your way through the floating ice blocks. There may be days when it is not possible to get very close to the front of **Le Conte Glacier**, but you can almost always get a view of it. *Caution:* In the summer there are many baby seals with their mothers on the ice flows. Avoid coming too close or frightening them. Babies that are separated from their mothers may perish.

Where to Stay

CAMPING Camping is permitted anywhere. However, campsites are hard to find in the upper part of the bay.

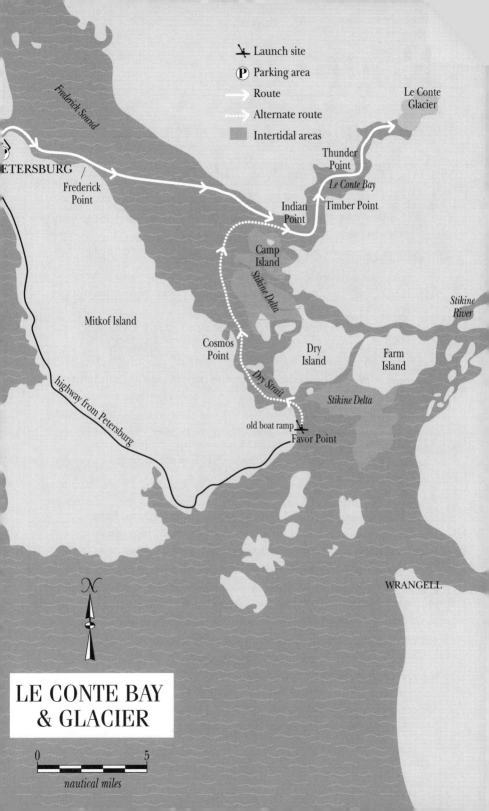

Launch site
Ⓟ Parking area
→ Route
⇢ Alternate route
Intertidal areas

Frederick Sound

Le Conte Glacier

ETERSBURG

Thunder Point

Frederick Point

Le Conte Bay

Indian Point

Timber Point

Camp Island

Stikine Delta

Mitkof Island

Cosmos Point

Stikine River

Dry Island

Farm Island

highway from Petersburg

Dry Strait

Stikine Delta

old boat ramp

Favor Point

WRANGELL

N

LE CONTE BAY & GLACIER

0   5

nautical miles

Route 8:

——————————————————————————⟶

Petersburg to Kake—Wrangell Narrows & Keku Strait

This fascinating trip is less difficult than it first appears. On it you pass through an assortment of beautiful settings and have the opportunity to see wildlife, including whales, porpoise, seals, and sea lions. You will cruise by black bears, river otters, mink, Sitka black-tailed deer, and if you are lucky, wolves on the shore. In July and August there are ample opportunities for picking blueberries and red huckleberries. Eagles and waterfowl are abundant. When I made this trip, there were loons everywhere.

TRIP HIGHLIGHTS: Varied topography, scenic views, and abundant wildlife. Rocky Pass in Keku Strait is typically a quiet and peaceful lake-like protected area.

TRIP RATING:
Intermediate/Advanced: This trip can be highly variable in complexity depending on the weather and therefore is recommended primarily for experienced paddlers. Less experienced kayakers will have a safe and fascinating time if accompanied by an experienced colleague, or if a kayak delivery service is used to avoid the sometimes difficult paddling in Sumner Strait.

TRIP DURATION: In very settled weather a strong paddler can make this trip comfortably in four days with three nights of camping along the way. A more leisurely trip in five or six days figures in some time for inclement weather. From Petersburg to Sumner Strait is 25 miles, and from there to the beginning of Keku Strait is 20 miles. The rest of the way to Kake is about 34 miles.

NAVIGATION AIDS: NOAA chart 17360 is adequate and easy to use while kayaking. For greater detail in Wrangell Narrows consider NOAA chart 17375. The Keku Strait portion will be more enjoyable if you have the U.S. Forest Service's *Kuiu Island Canoe/Kayak Routes.* NOAA chart 17372 also gives detailed coverage of Keku Strait. (Overall I consider NOAA chart 17360 the easiest to use while kayaking; see Appendix 3.)

TIDAL INFORMATION: Planning each day's paddling with the tides is important for both Wrangell Narrows and Rocky Pass and will save effort elsewhere.

CAUTIONS: Wrangell Narrows is a heavily trafficked waterway with a reputation for danger. But most of the way the narrows are wide enough that a kayaker who stays along the shore will be out of the way of the worst of the ships' wakes, which seem to be the major concern. It pays to check the ferry schedule before you go through the narrows. You'll want to be in a wide place when ferries pass. Ferry wakes could be dangerous if you happened to be in shallow water or on the shoreline.

Also the Sumner Strait portion of the trip, especially where you transition from Sumner Strait to Keku Strait, is a very open area that can receive full strength winds and seas moving north from the ocean.

TRIP PLANNING: Get a long-range weather forecast before you leave and have tide tables along. A weather radio is good equipment to bring. There is ferry service into Kake twice a week northbound and twice a week southbound. You may want to plan your trip to jibe with the ferry schedule. This trip can also be run in reverse just as well. There are north and south ferries passing through Petersburg nearly every day.

LAUNCH SITE: Leave from the small boat harbors in Petersburg or Kake. Otherwise it is possible to arrange for a powerboat to drop you off and/or pick you up somewhere along the way.

DIRECTIONS

Leave from Petersburg by heading south along Wrangell Narrows. **Green Point**, 7.0 miles from Petersburg, is the approximate null point location of Wrangell Narrows so it pays to arrive there at high tide. In settled weather this means leaving Petersburg about three hours before high tide. Continue south from Green Point with the beginning ebb so that it will take you through the narrowest point of the main channel. At **Burnt Island**, 6.5 miles farther, the Wrangell Narrows channel heads south, but you will turn southwest into **Keene Channel** on the north side of Keene Island, which leads into **Beecher Pass**. There are numerous houses in this area and camping is not recommended. Continue on through the pass or turn north into **Duncan Canal** where there are ample opportunities to set up your tent.

The trip continues south by the **Level Islands** and into **Sumner Strait**, then westward past **Mitchell Point, Douglas Bay, Moss Island**, to **Totem Bay**. Cross Totem Bay to **Totem Point** and **Yellow Point** then on to **Point Barrie** where you turn north into **Keku Strait**. From Mitchell Point west there are sufficient camping spots to choose from.

Moving north through beautiful Keku Strait and **Rocky Pass** will be much easier if you use the tide to push you along. This scenic area deserves a leisurely pace, and you will probably want to camp here as well. There is a null point in the vicinity of **The Summit** so arrive there near high tide. *Sidetrips:* There are a number of arms and bays along the way that bear exploring if time permits. Be sure to save some time for exploring among the many small islands in Rocky Pass.

Where to Stay

CAMPING   Attractive and scenic places to camp all along this route are abundant. The only exceptions are around the houses along Keene Channel and Beecher Pass and along a rather inhospitable looking stretch of shoreline between Duncan Canal and Mitchell Point. **FOREST SERVICE CABINS**   There are four cabins along this route (see Appendix 2).

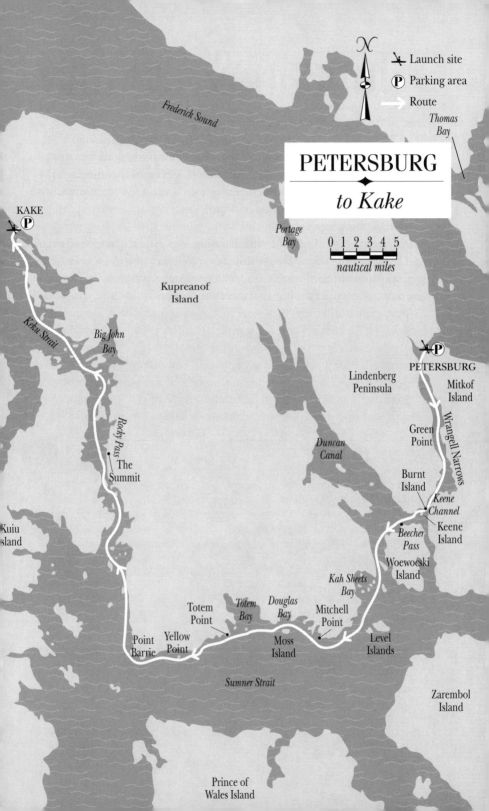

Juneau & Vicinity

I f you are coming from a metropolitan area in the lower 48, Juneau (30,240 population) will seem like a small town. However it is Southeast Alaska's largest and busiest city and the state capital. It is an important crossroad for kayakers who are on their way to other paddling destinations or who plan to begin trips here.

Juneau has anything and everything a kayaker might need, including boat rentals, outfitting, guided excursions, and kayak transportation services. There are numerous hotels and restaurants (including a bagel bakery that is second to none), a youth hostel, and two Forest Service campgrounds. It is also the hub of the Alaska Marine Highway ferry system. Alaska Airlines has plenty of flights in and out, and there are numerous floatplane services.

For the kayaker Juneau can be considered in two parts. The downtown area, including the town of Douglas, is the site of three marinas. This is where the cruise ships dock. From here you and your kayak can catch a ride to Tracy Arm. Paddling south in the Gastineau Channel, you can spend the day exploring, begin a trip around Douglas Island, or cross Stephens Passage to Oliver Inlet.

The rest of Juneau is the Auke Bay area 10 miles northwest of downtown. There is another boat harbor here as well as the docks for the AMHS and the Auk Nu ferries. The airport is 2.5 miles from Auke Bay.

Route 9:

━ ➤

Auke Bay & Mendenhall Bar Channel

Auke Bay is a good locale for beginning paddlers. It is relatively easy to put in at the boat harbor, and the bay is big enough and sufficiently varied to allow interesting paddling. These are generally protected waters, but if conditions do become unpleasant, it is easy to quit and go home.

Under favorable wind and tide conditions, the paddle from Auke Bay to downtown Juneau is an easy day trip through Mendenhall Bar Channel—the shallow upper reaches of Gastineau Channel.

TRIP HIGHLIGHTS: Spectacular view of Mendenhall Glacier. Opportunity to deal with shallow water paddling in a following current. Lots of eagles.

TRIP RATING:
Beginner: Inside Auke Bay learner level skills sufficient. From the bay to downtown is safe enough for newly hatched kayakers with the proviso that if any significant wind pipes up, they'll go ashore and wait for better conditions.

TRIP DURATION: In Auke Bay spend as much time as you want. The trip downtown covers a distance of 11 miles and will take you between five and six hours depending on tide and wind.

NAVIGATION AIDS: NOAA chart 17315 or USGS *Juneau* (B-2 and B-3).

TIDAL INFORMATION: Tide is important. The Mendenhall Bar Channel goes completely dry, and you will not be able to get through until about three and one-half hours after low tide. Once past the null point, however, the current is hardly noticeable when heading south.

CAUTIONS: In Auke Bay be alert for small boat traffic, especially inside the marina. If your tide timing is off when crossing Mendenhall Bar, be prepared for some short delays.

TRIP PLANNING: Make plans in accordance with an early morning low tide: Begin paddling from Auke Bay on the low or within a couple of hours after low tide. Get a weather forecast update before leaving Auke Bay. A light northerly wind will be to your liking.

LAUNCH SITE: Launch from Auke Bay Marina. Probably no one will bother you about a launch fee if you just carry your kayak down to the water, get in, and paddle away. Parking does require payment. (There is a convenience store at Auke Bay.)

DIRECTIONS

AUKE BAY: For day trips in **Auke Bay**, you can paddle most anywhere that you like from the marina while watching out for boats moving in and out of the marina. Appropriate caution is warranted near the ferry terminals on the bay's west side.

Auke Bay & Mendenhall Bar Channel

AUKE BAY TO DOWNTOWN JUNEAU: Favor the left (east) side of Auke Bay and exit the bay between **Spuhn Island** and **Smugglers Cove**. Enter **Fritz Cove**—you'll soon have a magnificent view of Mendenhall Glacier. Head southeast for **green marker 21** in order to pick up the channel. For the next 3.0 miles on a rising tide, it will be necessary to pay attention to stay in deep enough water. If you run out of water deep enough to float, just wait. In a few minutes the tide will "rise to the occasion." If it looks like you have a long wait, find a nice spot to picnic or rest. The vast sandy bars and flats are interesting to walk on, and footing is usually good. Just be sure your kayak is secured.

Once the shallow water is behind you, you are in Gastineau Channel. Although the tide will still be rising, the current will not usually be difficult to deal with. You will prefer the wind to be at your back, but commonly there is a breeze out of the south or southwest that may slow your progress. If a significant headwind picks up, you can go ashore most anywhere on the **Douglas Island** side and easily haul out.

Continue southeast along either shoreline of Gastineau Channel depending on your destination. But choose a preferred side early to avoid having to cross the channel later when there might be a crosswind. *Caution:* Strong currents are sometimes encountered under the **Juneau-Douglas Bridge**. Approach this area with care.

At the end of your trip, it is possible to land at **Harris Harbor** or **Aurora Basin**, which are just north of the bridge, or continue on another 3.5 miles to **Douglas Island Harbor**.

The trip from Auke Bay to Juneau can also be run in the other direction by starting out from Juneau or Douglas. (There is bus service every day between downtown Juneau, Douglas, and Auke Bay.) When winds are southerly it will be easier that way. Here again begin the trip on a flooding tide, starting out an hour or so after low tide.

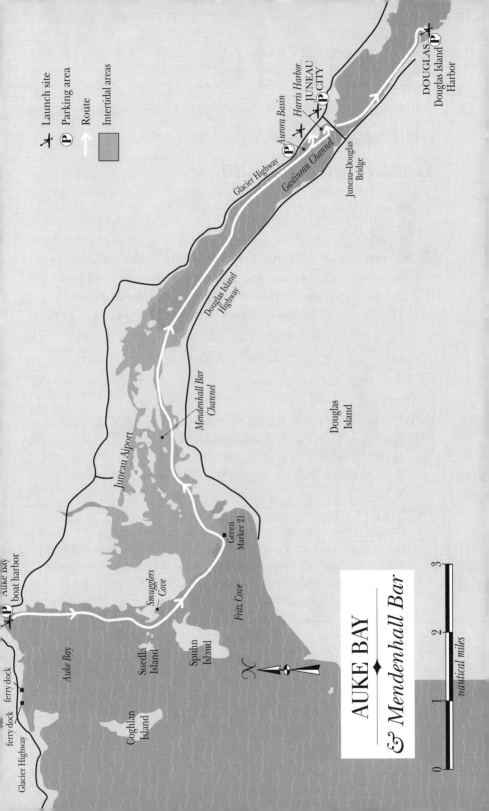

AUKE BAY & Mendenhall Bar

Launch site
Parking area
Route
Intertidal areas

nautical miles
0   1   2   3

Glacier Highway
ferry dock
ferry dock
Auke Bay boat harbor
Auke Bay
Coghlan Island
Suedla Island
Spuhn Island
Smugglers Cove
Green Marker 21
Fritz Cove
Juneau Airport
Mendenhall Bar Channel
Douglas Island Highway
Douglas Island
Glacier Highway
Gastineau Channel
Aurora Basin
Harris Harbor
JUNEAU CITY
Juneau-Douglas Bridge
DOUGLAS
Douglas Island Harbor

Route 10:

■■ ■■ ■■ ■■ ■■ ■■ ■■ ■■ ■■ ■■ ■■ ■■ ■■ ➤

Juneau/Douglas & Lower Gastineau Channel

Juneau and Douglas line the northeast and southwest
sides of Gastineau Channel. Paddling around the town
docks is of only questionable interest. On the Juneau side
there are huge cruise ships alongside the city docks or
anchored in the channel. Things are more peaceful on the
Douglas side. Farther down channel (southeast) on either
side, the density of commercial operations and homes drops
off rapidly, and you soon find yourself with a scenic
shoreline.

TRIP HIGHLIGHTS: In-town paddling can be fascinating if you are
interested in viewing the activities of fishing and commercial craft
close up. However this should be done with care (see Cautions).
Away from town cruising along the shoreline will offer many scenic
views.

TRIP RATING:

Beginner/Intermediate: For the beginner the Douglas side is a better
place to practice and improve your skills. There is boat traffic, but
no floatplanes to worry about. Here too there is plenty of room
outside of the navigation channel to explore. On the Juneau side
there is a lot of small boat, cruise ship, sightseeing boat, fishing
vessel, and at times dense floatplane traffic. It is not difficult
paddling, but it does demand attention at all times.

TRIP DURATION: Trips along the waterfronts of Juneau and
Douglas can take a few hours or a half day. Continuing down the
channel to Pt. Salisbury and Bishop Point and to Marmion Island
and back is a round-trip of about 16 to 22 miles and will require six
to eight hours.

NAVIGATION AIDS: NOAA chart 17315.

TIDAL INFORMATION: Juneau area tide ranges can be as much as 24 feet; typical summer tides range between 14 and 20 feet. Be prepared to deal with flood and ebb tidal currents in Gastineau Channel. Plan your trip with the tides in mind to avoid expending a lot of unnecessary energy fighting the flow.

CAUTIONS: Under the Juneau-Douglas Bridge, currents can be somewhat strong, and they move in variable directions. Farther down Gastineau Channel use great care around the cruise ship docks: Floatplanes land here and sometimes cannot see kayaks, ship bow thrusters can produce unexpected side wakes, and lighters operating between anchored cruise ships and the dock are notorious for ignoring kayakers.

TRIP PLANNING: Consult the tide table to get some extra help along the way. If you go as far as Bishop Point or Marmion Island, make the trip using the tide flow. Just before getting underway, get a current weather forecast. There are plenty of places where it is easy to haul out along Gastineau Channel.

Juneau/Douglas & Lower Gastineau Channel

LAUNCH SITE: The easiest launch sites are Harris Harbor, Aurora Basin, or the Douglas Island Harbor. If you are planning to head southeast on Gastineau Channel, avoid the commercial hubbub of the Juneau side and use Douglas Island Harbor. Free parking at all boat harbors.

DIRECTIONS

For Juneau and Douglas area trips and for day trips along **Gastineau Channel**, it is simply a matter of following the shore to the southeast or northwest. Gastineau Channel is about 1.0 mile wide. At times there is a lot of boat traffic. Neophyte kayakers will be better off avoiding crossings by sticking to one side or the other for day trips. *Sidetrip:* The trip down Gastineau Channel and the transit between Auke Bay and Downtown Juneau/Douglas can also be part of a Douglas Island circumnavigation taking three or four days. This scenic trip offers adequate camping around the island and opportunities to see whales and a variety of waterfowl. Be warned however that this is an adventure for experienced paddlers, and anyone with minimal skills should definitely be accompanied by a guide or experienced friend. Half of the trip is in Stephens Passage, which can mean rough water with strong winds and significant waves. In settled weather it is an easy trip, but conditions change fast here. Experienced Juneau kayakers say anyone doing it should be savvy enough to know when to haul out and take time to let conditions improve.

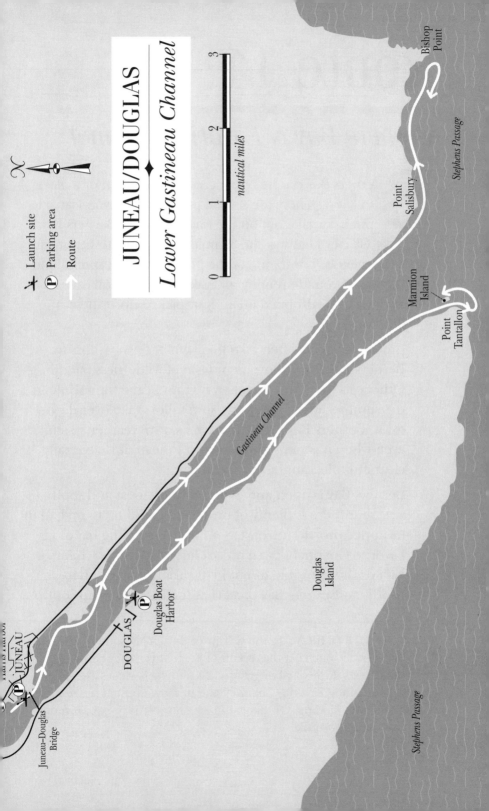

JUNEAU/DOUGLAS
Lower Gastineau Channel

Launch site
Ⓟ Parking area
→ Route

0   1   2   3
nautical miles

Juneau–Douglas Bridge

JUNEAU

DOUGLAS

Douglas Boat Harbor

Gastineau Channel

Douglas Island

Marmion Island

Point Tantallon

Point Salisbury

Bishop Point

Stephens Passage

Stephens Passage

Route 11:

---------- ---------- ----------➤

Berners Bay & Favorite Channel

Berners Bay can be considered a destination or a place to kayak. There are several places along Lynn Canal to put in or take out on the way to or from Berners Bay. Take Glacier Highway the 39 miles from downtown Juneau to Berners Bay or to one of the put-in/take-out spots along the way. If you are renting a kayak in Juneau, you can arrange to be dropped off and/or picked up at these locations.

Juneau kayakers often take their out-of-town visitors to Berners Bay for a convenient taste of wilderness paddling. Others go there just to get away from home for a while in the summer when the cruise ship sailors take over downtown. Berners Bay seems to have its own weather system; even when it is rainy and blowy in Juneau, it is generally clear and pleasant out near the bay.

Berners Bay is open and exposed to the west and southwest, but there is plenty of protected paddling to be had in its upper (northern) part. Southward from the bay along Favorite Channel lies an area referred to as the Channel Islands. It is possible to put in at various harbors here and paddle to Berners Bay or start at the bay and head south.

TRIP HIGHLIGHTS: In the vicinity of Berners Bay, there are a lot of eagles to watch. At the mouth of Eagle River, they congregate by the dozens. Individual or groups of humpback whales are generally present along Favorite Channel, and it is not unusual to see them bubble-net feeding. On Benjamin Island there is the opportunity to visit a sea lion rookery.

TRIP RATING:

> *Beginner/Intermediate:* For those who have very little experience there is protected paddling at Echo Cove. In settled conditions relatively inexperienced paddlers can also paddle north or south between the launch points or even as far south as Auke Bay. *Caution:* Paddling in and out of Eagle River campground is usually safe only for experienced paddlers who can deal with the strong currents.

TRIP DURATION: You can spend an afternoon or several days in Berners Bay. A trip from Berners Bay to Auke Bay combined with some island camping could take two to four or even five days, with the option to stop at one of the launch point harbors along the way. I have made the trip from Amelga Harbor to Echo Cove in about six and one-half hours of steady but not strenuous paddling on a light air day. Echo Cove to the head of Berners Bay is 9 miles. From Amelga Harbor to Echo Cove is 17.5 miles, and from Tee Harbor to Echo Cove is 21 miles.

NAVIGATION AIDS: NOAA chart 17316 or 17300.

TIDAL INFORMATION: Juneau tides have maximums of 24 feet, with typical summer ranges of 14 to 20 feet.

CAUTIONS: Monitor the weather and head for shore when the winds or seas pick up. When paddling by Benjamin Island stay on the east side or at least one-quarter mile off the beach on the west side This is a sea lion haul out and the animals should not be hassled. (A better program is to beach your kayak on the south end of the island and hike the forest trail up the southwest side to a cliff that overlooks the sea lion haul out.)

TRIP PLANNING: The last convenience store is at Auke Bay. Water may be at a premium along this route. If you plan to camp on the islands, bring a good supply. If you decide to put in at one location and take out at another, have someone arrange to pick you up at your destination or leave a vehicle at your arrival place. Hitchhiking is a reasonable option and most drivers will give you a lift, but be prepared to wait because few cars pass this way.

LAUNCH SITES: From Auke Bay to Berners Bay there are five possible launch sites for kayaking: First is Auke Bay boat harbor (see Rte. 9). Next is Tee Harbor (6.2 miles by road from Auke Bay Marina). Here you can launch from a state-sponsored beach. To

get there turn left off Glacier Highway at the Tee Harbor turn sign, then take the immediate right turn. The road goes to a gravel beach that is a launch point. Limited parking is available.

Amelga Harbor is shown on some maps as Dotsons Landing. Follow the road 12.2 miles from Auke Bay Marina. Note there is no sign on the highway, but there is a paved road off to the left as you drive north. Amelga Harbor is at the end of this side road approximately 0.5 mile from the highway. This is a state harbor with a ramp. Walk down the ramp or down the stairs to the right of the ramp and launch from the mixed rock-gravel-mud beach. Parking is available as are rest rooms.

Next is Eagle River Campground, 14.8 road miles from Auke Bay Marina. The only indication that there is a campground is a parking sign on the highway. At this location you will launch right into the Eagle River, and because of the very swift current, you must use maximum caution. (I did not like the looks of it and went elsewhere.) If you launch here, be sure it is at high tide and keep control of your boat. Be especially cautious here with children. Pay parking, rest rooms, and campsites are available.

Berners Bay & Favorite Channel

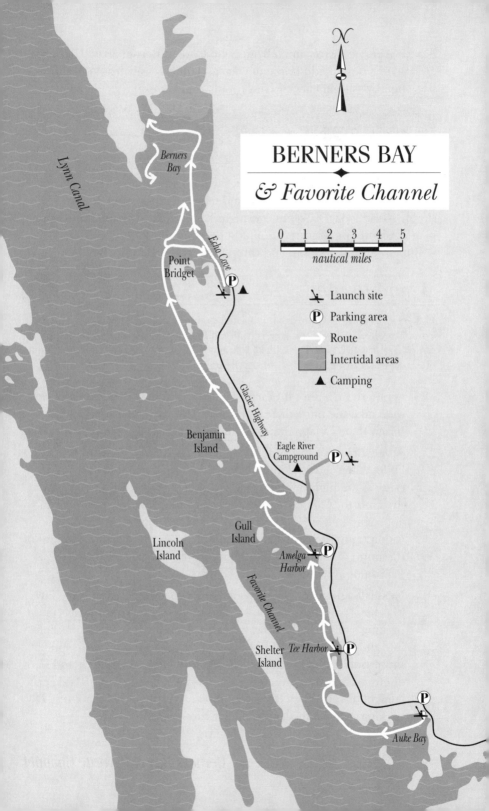

It is very easy to launch from Echo Cove at Berners Bay. There is a state maintained ramp, but you can launch easily from the shore nearby as well. Parking, rest rooms, and campsites available here.

DIRECTIONS

The routes to **Berners Bay** from the various launch sites are suggestions only. It is not unrealistic to put in and take out at the same location and simply spend a day, make an overnight kayak-camping trip to one of the nearby islands, or select a camping spot along the shoreline. You have as well the option to explore and camp throughout Berners Bay.

Where to Stay

CAMPING   There are established campgrounds at Eagle Creek and Echo Cove. Elsewhere most of the area is National Forest, and there is no restriction on camping.   **FOREST CABINS**   There is a National Forest and a state of Alaska cabin in Berners Bay (see Appendix 2).

Route 12:

■ ■ ■ ■ ■ ■ ■ ■ ■ ■ ■ ■ ■ ■ ■ ➤

Tracy Arm

racy Arm is the low-budget version of Glacier Bay. It attracts quite a few kayakers every summer. The sheer cliffs of the fjord offer incredible views but few places to camp. Those who elect to paddle the approximately 30 miles from Holkham Bay to South Sawyer Glacier will usually experience protected waters most of the way. However there is a lot of boat traffic, and the attendant noise and wakes detract somewhat from the grandeur of the place.

TRIP HIGHLIGHTS: Opportunity to kayak in a steep-walled fjord and visit tidal glaciers. Wildlife viewing with main emphasis on seals and likelihood of seeing bears any time and mountain goats in May and June.

TRIP RATING AND DURATION:
Beginner/Intermediate: Complexity and duration depends on where your trip begins and ends. For example, if you are dropped off and picked up by a delivery boat in Upper Tracy Arm, the generally calm conditions make for easy paddling. Those paddling the full distance from or to Juneau need to be experienced (see Launch Site following).

NAVIGATION AIDS: NOAA chart 17300 or USGS *Sumdum, Alaska-Canada* at 1:250,000.

TIDAL INFORMATION: Tracy Arm and adjacent Endicott Arm meet at Holkham Bay. The entrance to either arm is characterized by very strong currents on ebb and flood tidal cycles. When entering either arm, it is necessary to take advantage of slack water and to stay out of the main channel. Fords Terror is a small scenic fjord off Endicott Arm famous for its awesome currents at low water. Entering it at high slack however is not difficult.

CAUTIONS: Tidal features are cause for caution. Exercise caution near the face of the tidal glaciers (see Glaciers, page 31). Remember too that Tracy Arm is a popular spot for boats and ships that often create significant wakes.

There is usually a dense pack of floating ice blocks in the upper parts of Endicott Arm, moving in response to wind and tide. It is possible to become trapped in the ice if it moves in behind you. Keep in mind the wind and tide conditions and be ready to head out quickly.

TRIP PLANNING: Most important is to plan your paddling with the tides in mind and stay aware of what is going on around you. In Tracy Arm and Endicott Arm, the fjord walls rise steeply from the water, and you often have to paddle miles between possible haul out points.

LAUNCH SITE: Where you launch from will determine the difficulty of your trip to Tracy Arm and the amount of skill you will need. It is possible to paddle from Juneau to Tracy Arm and vicinity, but this is a long trip that is very weather dependent. A more popular option is to catch a ride with one of the delivery services or daily excursion boats from Juneau to the Tracy Arm glaciers or almost any place you want to go in the fjord. They will pick you up at the same or another location one or more days later. Using this popular option means that your trip will be mostly in protected waters.

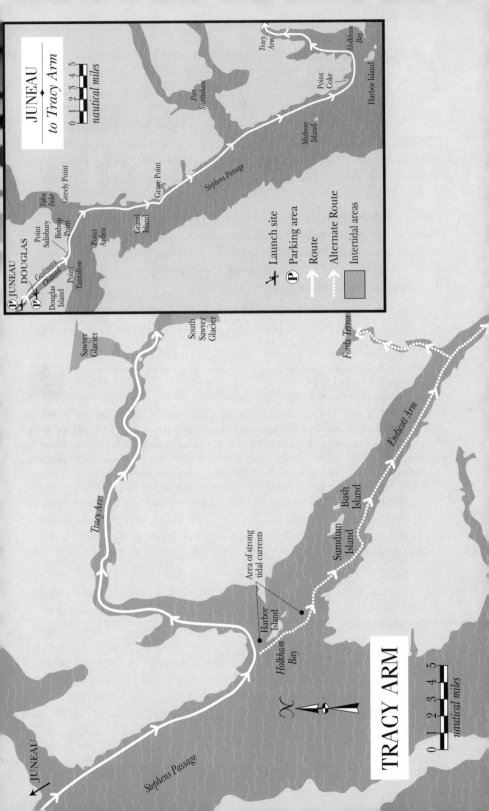

JUNEAU
to Tracy Arm

0 1 2 3 4 5
nautical miles

JUNEAU
DOUGLAS

Point Salisbury
Bishop Point
Gastineau Channel
Douglas Island
Point Tantallon
Point Arden

Taku Inlet
Greely Point
Grave Point

Grand Island

Stephens Passage

Port Snettisham

Midway Island
Point Coke

Tracy Arm
Holkham Bay

Harbor Island

Launch site
Parking area
Route
Alternate Route
Intertidal areas

TRACY ARM

0 1 2 3 4 5
nautical miles

JUNEAU

Sawyer Glacier

South Sawyer Glacier

Fords Terror

Tracy Arm

Endicott Arm

Bush Island

Sumdum Island

Area of strong tidal currents

Harbor Island

Holkham Bay

Stephens Passage

DIRECTIONS

Those leaving from Juneau will proceed southeast down **Gastineau Channel** to **Stephens Passage**, cross **Taku Inlet**, and continue southeast to **Holkham Bay**. Once at Holkham Bay proceed east, then north up Tracy Arm or continue southeast to **Endicott Arm**, paying close attention to the tides.

Caution: If leaving from Douglas or from Juneau stay on the east side of Gastineau and Stephens to avoid open-water crossings. Stephens Passage is often difficult paddling. Crossing Taku Inlet can be extremely hazardous when there is an east wind. Don't push your luck on this one. Just haul out and wait for better conditions.

Sidetrips: At Holkam Bay it is possible to turn southeast to explore Endicott Arm and Fords Terror. Campsites are few and haulout points can be miles apart.

Where to Stay

CAMPING   All of the area is designated National Forest or National Wilderness so it is possible to camp anywhere. In Tracy Arm and Endicott Arm, there are few campsites. Most popular are the mouths of the valleys, one on each side of Tracy Arm, about 17 miles from Harbor Island. It is apparently also possible to camp farther on at the mouth of the valley on the south side of Tracy Arm between South Sawyer Glacier and the inlet into Sawyer Glacier.

Route 13:

----------------------------➤

Oliver Inlet & Seymour Canal

The Oliver Inlet/Seymour Canal trip is is one of Southeast Alaska's most popular extended tours, and although you are likely to see other kayakers along the way now and then, it is still a remote get-away-from-it-all sort of adventure. Expect to see plenty of wildlife: Humpbacks and orcas ply the waters of Seymour Canal and seals are abundant. Loons, crows, ravens, common mergansers, and many, many murrelets and scoters will be around you much of the time. This area is part of Admiralty Island, which is renown for the dense populations of brown bears and eagles. Between Oliver Inlet and Seymour Canal, there is a roller coaster tramway on which to transport your kayak(s).

In late June and into July, there will be lots of salmonberries and blueberries to enjoy. Paddling in Seymour Canal is very scenic, with snow-capped mountains in the background. There are lots of bays and islands to explore and camping spots are easy to find—some choice spots are on picturesque islands. The bear observatory at Pack Creek and a hiking trail at Mole Harbor are popular destinations. *Caution:* The most difficult part of the trip is crossing Stephens Passage between Gastineau Channel and Oliver Inlet. Crossing Stephens Passage is serious business, and you should absolutely expect and be prepared to wait on either side if necessary. This is an open-water crossing of one to two hours for experienced kayakers. It is often very rough in Stephens Passage, and every year it seems that significant accidents happen to kayakers here. Time, tide, and weather figure heavily in the crossing. Generally the best time to cross is early in the morning or sometimes in the evening. You can easily eliminate this part of the trip by using one of the kayak delivery services from Juneau.

TRIP HIGHLIGHTS: Wildlife viewing, excellent scenery, remote campsites, and the portage tramway.

TRIP RATING:

Intermediate/Advanced: Depending on how you arrange logistics, this can be a trip for experienced paddlers only or for those of moderate experience and/or beginners if accompanied by experienced colleagues.

TRIP DURATION: For a worthwhile adventure plan on at least five or six days in Seymour Canal. Those who paddle all the way from and to Juneau will want to add two more days to this as well as having a flexible return time if they have to wait for favorable conditions in Stephens Passage.

If you paddle all the way from Douglas to Pack Creek, for example, it is a round-trip of about 27 miles. With a transport service between Juneau and Oliver Inlet on both ends of the trip, paddling is reduced to about 18 miles.

NAVIGATION AIDS: NOAA chart 17300. (Also bring along chart 17360 if you plan to paddle into lower Seymour Canal.)

TIDAL INFORMATION: Tide range is as described for Auke Bay route (Rte. 9). Paddling from Juneau to Oliver Inlet will be a lot easier and faster if the trip is planned with the tides in mind. Working with the tides is critical for Oliver Inlet and for Seymour Canal (see Directions).

CAUTIONS: Main cautions are crossing Stephens Passage, currents in Oliver Inlet, and care with the tramcar—all of which are described.

TRIP PLANNING: The most important factor in long-range planning is to pick days with tides running in the direction most convenient for you to get you through Oliver Inlet and across the tramway at a convenient time. Just before setting out get an updated short- and long-term weather forecast. Leave your proposed route and itinerary with someone in Juneau. A VHF radio is a good companion here.

LAUNCH SITE: Same as for Rte. 10 from Juneau and Douglas.

Oliver Inlet & Seymour Canal

Portage logistics will provide the fun and games on this trip. The challenges are (a) paddling through Oliver Inlet, (b) using the tramway car between Oliver Inlet and Seymour Canal, and (c) getting underway into Seymour Canal at high tide.

Once you arrive at the entrance to Oliver Inlet, there are two tide-dependent factors to consider. One is paddling through the inlet, and the other is being in Seymour Canal and ready to go on the exact top of the high tide. Executing this takes some skill, planning, and luck because it includes moving your gear via the tramway, unloading it, and carrying it down the water on the Seymour Canal side. If everything goes well, it will be a three-to-four-hour operation.

For about half of the tidal cycle you'll encounter rough white water at the Oliver Inlet entrance. At low tide there are rocks to be reckoned with. The best time to make it through Oliver is at about three and one-half to four hours before high tide. Once through the inlet entrance, it is about a thirty-minute paddle to the tramway that crosses to Seymour. Note that some maps and charts show a portage trail. This is not the location of the tramway. The tram is at the head of the inlet bay. It is obvious by a large sign on shore.

If the tramcar is not there, it is necessary to walk over to the Seymour Canal side and push it back. The tramway is about 1.0-mile long. The car and tracks are sometimes in rather poor condition. For example, the hand brakes may be broken. If so your only choice is to proceed very slowly and figure out how to stop the car on the downgrades. The board path between the rails may be missing boards, so choose your steps carefully. On the Oliver Inlet side, the car should not go farther then the top of the hill. Rails running down to the water are broken and attempts to use them will cause the car to derail.

Once you and your load of gear reach the Seymour Canal side of the tram, you may still have as much as a third of a mile to haul your gear, depending on the tide. The higher the tide, the easier it will be. Even a 14-foot high tide means lugging stuff a long way; it may be worthwhile to camp and wait for a better tide. At low tide the head of Seymour Canal is a broad shallow tidal flat as much as 1.0 mile wide. If possible choose a tide of 16 feet or more and plan to have your kayak loaded and ready to

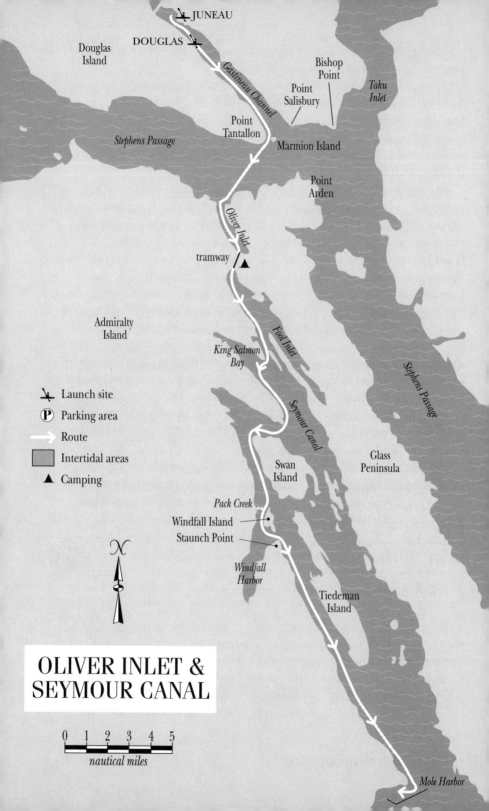

JUNEAU

DOUGLAS

Douglas
Island

Gastineau Channel

Point
Tantallon

Stephens Passage

Bishop
Point

Point
Salisbury

*Taku
Inlet*

Marmion Island

Point
Arden

Oliver Inlet

tramway ▲

Pool Inlet

*King Salmon
Bay*

Admiralty
Island

Seymour Canal

Stephens Passage

Swan
Island

Glass
Peninsula

Pack Creek

Windfall Island

Staunch Point

*Windfall
Harbor*

Tiedeman
Island

Launch site

Ⓟ Parking area

Route

Intertidal areas

▲ Camping

N

**OLIVER INLET &
SEYMOUR CANAL**

0   1   2   3   4   5
nautical miles

Mole Harbor

depart into Seymour Canal exactly at high tide. (Heading back to Juneau the reverse logistics apply.)

Those who paddle from a Juneau or Douglas launch will proceed southeast down **Gastineau Channel** (see Rte. 10). After rounding **Marmion Island** and **Point Tantallon** on the southeast corner of Douglas Island, head slightly southwest to Oliver Inlet with due regard for sea conditions. With the appropriate tide proceed through Oliver Inlet to the tramway.

Once in the water at the head of **Seymour Canal**, you can paddle southeast as you wish. There are ample opportunities to explore a variety of bays and inlets. If going to **Pack Creek** or **Mole Harbor**, your route can follow the shoreline of **Admiralty Island** and pass on either side of Swan Island to arrive at the Pack Creek ranger station on the north end of **Windfall Island**. *Sidetrips:* The most popular attraction of Seymour Canal is Pack Creek, a state managed bear-watching area. There is usually little bear activity at Pack Creek until early July. From then until the end of August reservations are often booked far in advance. From the viewing area it is possible to watch and photograph bears catching salmon. In the summer this is a fee area, and only a limited number of people are allowed to visit each day. Reservations have to be made and paid for well in advance (phone 907–588–8790). The down side of the popularity of Pack Creek is that there is a constant stream of floatplanes that fly there every day, and their incessant drone detracts somewhat from your "wilderness experience."

King Salmon Bay, Swan Bay, Windfall Harbor, Fool Inlet, and Mole Harbor are all fascinating places to explore by kayak. Even if you don't go to Pack Creek, you are almost sure to see brown bears somewhere along the shore in these areas.

Where to Stay

CAMPING   If it is necessary to wait for the tide at Oliver Inlet or for improving conditions before crossing Stephens Passage, it is easy to camp at the entrance to Oliver Inlet. On the Seymour Canal side of the tramway, there is a campsite adjacent to an Alaska State Parks cabin (see Appendix 2). Once in Seymour Canal there are many places to camp. If you are nervous about the bears, some of the islands may feel more comfortable. At Pack Creek on Windfall Island, the Alaska Department of Fish and Game has designated two free campsites. Get advice from the rangers at their camp on the north end of the island.

Oliver Inlet & Seymour Canal

Haines
& Vicinity

Haines is tucked away at the top of Lynn Canal in one of Southeast Alaska's most beautiful settings. Haines (population 2,400) is the only kayaking town in Southeast Alaska with a highway connection. It is served by the Alaska Marine Highway ferry and the Auk Nu ferry in and out of Juneau, as well as by charter floatplanes and small commercial land planes.

Haines is a town most travelers only expect to pass through because of its highway-waterway connections. However once you discover its beauty, it will be hard to leave. The town is surrounded by snow-draped mountain peaks laced with wispy patches of drifting clouds. In spite of an increasing tourist influx, it has managed to maintain its small town informality and friendliness.

Haines has several hotels, a youth hostel, restaurants, and grocery stores. Camping is available at Chilkoot Lake State Park, which is 9 miles east of town, or Chilkat State Park 7 miles southeast of town.

Route 14:

Chilkoot Lake

Chilkoot Lake is Haines's most unique kayaking venue. Chilkoot Lake almost always offers protected paddling and is an excellent place for inexperienced kayakers to practice. There is camping at Chilkoot Lake State Park near the kayak put-in location.

Kayakers will see lots of eagles around the lake, and it is a good place to watch bears during summer when salmon are spawning.

TRIP HIGHLIGHTS: Peaceful paddling under most wind conditions; an opportunity to view a variety of wildlife.

TRIP RATING: *Beginner:* Kayakers of *any level* of experience will enjoy the peaceful paddling here. It is an especially good place for practicing basic skills.

TRIP DURATION: This is an opportunity for a half- or full day of kayaking. A complete trip around the lake in a leisurely manner will take about five hours, but shorter excursions are easily done.

NAVIGATION AIDS: USGS topo map *Skagway* (B-2) covers the area. However the lake is small enough that a map is not really needed.

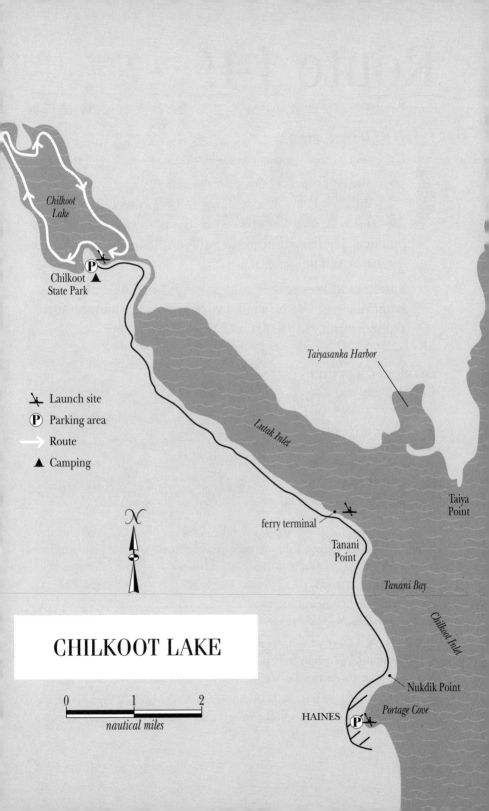

Chilkoot
Lake

Chilkoot
State Park

Taiyasanka Harbor

Ludak Inlet

N

Launch site

P Parking area

Route

▲ Camping

Taiya
Point

ferry terminal

Tanani
Point

Tanani Bay

Chilkoot Inlet

CHILKOOT LAKE

Nukdik Point

Portage Cove

HAINES

0   1   2
nautical miles

Chilkat and Chilkoot

Chilkat and Chilkoot sound a lot alike, but their difference is important if you are trying to find your way around Haines. Things to the east are Chilkoot and things to the west are Chilkat. It turns out that Chilkat means "many fish" and Chilkoot means "big fish." According to local people that designation is correct, but they hasten to add that all of the fish are great eating.

CAUTIONS: There are practically no cautions to concern paddlers here. Like any place in Southeast Alaska, kayakers must be careful to not startle bears that may be fishing along the shore.

TRIP PLANNING: Check the weather forecast. You can usually paddle here any time during the day. However early mornings are always the most peaceful.

LAUNCH SITE: Chilkoot State Park is 9 miles north of Haines along a paved road. Facilities include a ramp, floating dock, free parking lot, picnic shelter, and rest rooms.

DIRECTIONS

Once you are in your kayak on the lake, there is no prescribed route to follow. Most folks enjoy following along the shoreline with opportunities to see eagles and in late summer brown bears fishing for salmon where creeks enter the lake.

Where to Stay

CAMPING A state park campground is adjacent to the launch area.

Route 15:

━━ ━━ ━━ ━ ━━ ━━ ━ ━━ ━━ ━━ ━━ ━━ ━━ ━━ ━━ ➤

Lutak Inlet & Taiyasanka Harbor

Lutak Inlet and Taiyasanka Harbor provide scenic paddling at any time of the summer, but their main attribute is the opportunity to see a lot of marine mammals in the spring during heavy fish runs.

TRIP HIGHLIGHTS: Lutak Inlet is especially spectacular in the spring when sea lions, humpbacks whales, and orcas come here for the Eulachon run.

TRIP RATING:

Beginner/Intermediate: Most of this area is easy paddling in settled weather. On the south side of the inlet, there is a highway and other commercial development, which distracts from the enjoyment of wilderness but means easy access to shore for haul outs. In contrast the north side of Lutak Inlet has a steeper and more difficult shoreline. This area as well as Taiyasanka Harbor is a trip to be made with or by more experienced kayakers.

TRIP DURATION: Half- and full day.

NAVIGATION AIDS: NOAA chart 17317.

TIDAL INFORMATION: Excursions up and down the inlet are easier if you use the tides. Otherwise this is all deep water and not difficult to negotiate.

CAUTIONS: Be prepared to haul out if strong winds develop, especially in the area between Nukdik Point and Tanani Point . Where Lutak Inlet opens to Chilkoot Inlet take special care as this area is notorious for wind, waves, and difficult paddling.

TRIP PLANNING: Obtain a good weather forecast and include the tide schedule in your plans. In general this area is not recommended for overnight trips and camping. The south side of the inlet is largely privately owned, the north side is steep and lacks

good campsites. The land area around Taiyasanka Harbor has special significance to Native Americans in this area and is better left undisturbed.

LAUNCH SITE: Most paddlers launch from Portage Cove in Haines. It is also possible to put in along the road to the west of Tanani Point. Doing so is recommended for inexperienced paddlers. For some it will be convenient to put in at one location and take out at another along the road.

DIRECTIONS

Those starting out from **Portage Cove** in Haines follow the shoreline north across **Tanani Bay** to **Lutak Inlet** and then continue northwest along the inlet or cross over to the north side to **Taiyasanka Harbor**. Those putting in along the road on the south side of Lutak Inlet can proceed west toward the head of the inlet or cross to the north depending on level of experience.

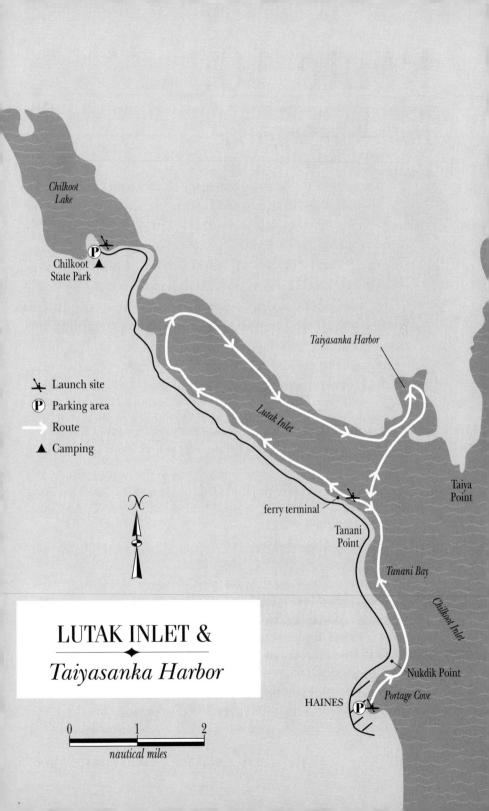

Chilkoot
Lake

Chilkoot
State Park

Taiyasanka Harbor

Launch site
Parking area
Route
Camping

Lutak Inlet

Taiya
Point

ferry terminal

Tanani
Point

Tanani Bay

Chilkoot Inlet

N

LUTAK INLET &
Taiyasanka Harbor

Nukdik Point

HAINES

Portage Cove

0   1   2
nautical miles

Route 16:

--→

Haines to Skagway

The Haines to Skagway trip appeals to a lot of folks, but it should only be attempted by experienced kayakers. The distance is not great, only about 17 miles, but the way is not always kayaker friendly. It *is* a scenic trip going either north or south through a fjord with views of snowfields and distant glaciers. The abrupt walls that rise from the waters of Taiya Inlet offer few opportunities to haul out or camp. This can be a problem because the constricted topography tends to focus winds, making for challenging paddling. It is quite reasonable to paddle one way and use the Auk Nu or the AMHS ferry for the other half of the trip.

TRIP HIGHLIGHTS: Scenic views—especially Sawmill Creek Waterfall, which cascades down the east side of Taiya Inlet across from Taiya Point.

TRIP RATING:
Intermediate/Advanced: For experienced kayakers due to possibility of strong winds and seas.

TRIP DURATION: One day each way.

NAVIGATION AIDS: NOAA chart 17317.

TIDAL INFORMATION: Tides here can reach 25 feet with summer maximums typically around 20 feet. Currents are not dangerous, but it pays to arrange to be paddling with the help of tidal currents. If you do find it necessary to camp on this route, pick your site with due respect to the tide.

CAUTIONS: Caution must be exercised when the wind pipes up, especially if wind and tide are opposed. Dominant summer wind is from the south. It tends to increase as the day wears on. Be especially prudent in the crossing of Lutak Inlet from Tanani Point

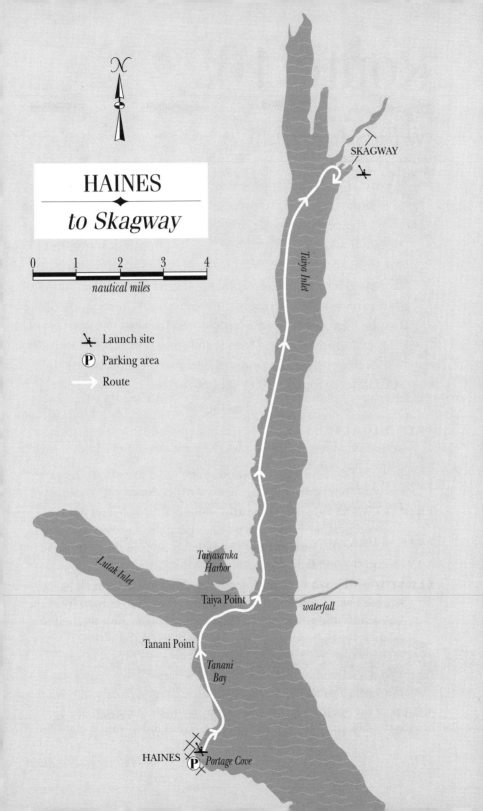

to Taiya Point. Strong winds and rough water are often encountered here, challenging even experienced kayakers.

TRIP PLANNING: Plan your trip with the tide table and get an updated weather forecast as often as possible. Kayakers are urged to pick the day carefully to be reasonably assured they can make it in one day due to limited camping possibilities.

LAUNCH SITE: It is possible to launch from the small boat harbor, but the usual—and much easier—procedure is to launch from the beach at Portage Cove. Parking is available near the cove.

DIRECTIONS

From **Portage Cove** head north across Lutak Inlet to **Taiya Point** and continue north up Taiya Inlet to **Skagway**.

Route 17:

━━ ━━ ━━ ━━ ━━ ━━ ━━ ━━ ━━ ━━ ━━ ➔

Chilkat Inlet

In the Chilkat Inlet area there are a variety of paddling destinations in a very scenic setting of forests and glaciers and snowy peaks in the background. Along shore there is the possibility of seeing bears. Eagles and waterfowl are always present. Whales, seals, and porpoises are often present in the inlet.

TRIP HIGHLIGHTS: Scenic paddling, glaciers, hiking, and viewing wildlife.

TRIP RATING:
Beginner/Intermediate: Paddling along the east side of the inlet is OK for those with limited skill and experience. Those crossing the inlet to Davidson Glacier should be more experienced or accompanied by experienced kayakers.

TRIP DURATION: Paddling in Chilkat Inlet can be part of half-, full-day, overnight or even multinight trips. The distance to Davidson Glacier for instance is 6 miles from the dock at Letnikof Cove.

NAVIGATION AIDS: NOAA chart 17317.

TIDAL INFORMATION: Tides in the Haines vicinity can reach a maximum of 25 feet, but summer tides are typically around 20 feet. This tide range is an important consideration when selecting a haul-out and camping site. Paddling along shore will be easier with an assist from the tide flow. At the head of the inlet, the large intertidal areas are best avoided.

CAUTIONS: In Chilkat Inlet winds can come up suddenly and produce difficult paddling conditions. Waters west and south of Kalhagu Cove can get especially rough. Waters off Seduction Point are well known for posing threats to all small craft. Be prepared to head for shore if necessary.

TRIP PLANNING: Obtain an up-to-date weather forecast with special attention to predicted winds. Take the opportunity to talk to local kayakers for advice on current conditions. The folks at Deishu Expeditions (see Appendix 1) are always willing to give advice to visitors.

LAUNCH SITE: Small boat harbor at Letnikof Cove or Chilkat State Park on Chilkat Peninsula.

DIRECTIONS

From either put-in point, you can travel north or south along the shore on the west side of **Chilkat Peninsula** for a few hours of paddling or a day trip. To the north lies **Pyramid Island**; south of **Letnikof Cove** is **Kochu Island**. The more adventurous can head across the inlet to **Green Point** or **Anchorage Point**, then south along the shore to **Glacier Point** with the opportunity for camping and a hike to **Davidson Glacier**. This trip can be an overnighter or extend to several days of camping, kayaking, and hiking on the glacial outwash deposits.

Where to Stay

CAMPING There are ample camping locations on the west side of Chilkat Inlet. On Chilkat Peninsula camp at Chilkat State Park.

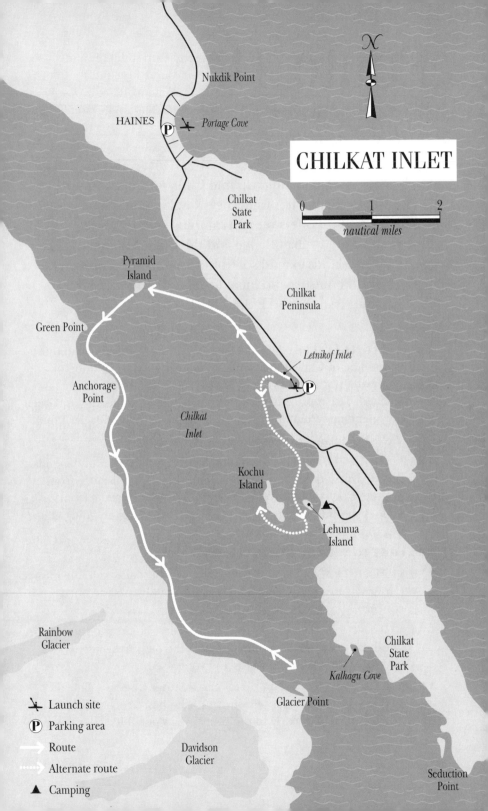

Route 18:

Chilkat Islands

This is a fascinating trip into Chilkoot Inlet and upper Lynn Canal. It is wilderness kayaking on seldom-visited islands. It offers remote camping with incredible scenic views of the Chilkat Range and the Coast Mountains. The Chilkat Islands extend south from Seduction Point on Chilkat Peninsula and include Talsani, Anyaka, Shikosi, Katagun Islands, and Eldred Rock.

TRIP HIGHLIGHTS: Wildlife viewing, unique wilderness island camping, and excellent mountain scenery.

TRIP RATING:
Advanced: For experienced kayakers. Those with limited experience should always be accompanied by a qualified guide. Winds and waves in the area can be awesome.

TRIP DURATION: This is a multiday trip whose duration depends on departure point and weather conditions. The distance from Portage Cove to Eldred Rock is 18 miles. Those leaving from Haines should budget at least five days if planning on going all the way to Eldred Rock and return.

NAVIGATION AIDS: NOAA chart 17317.

TIDAL INFORMATION: Use tidal flow to aid daily paddling efforts. Otherwise this is all deep water and intertidal areas are not a concern.

CAUTIONS: Plan all passages to and between islands with the wind in mind. Be prepared to modify or abort the day's activities as necessary for increasing winds and rough seas.

TRIP PLANNING: Get an up-to-date weather forecast. Take a VHF/weather radio along with you. The best procedure is to begin your trip as early in the morning as possible. That way if

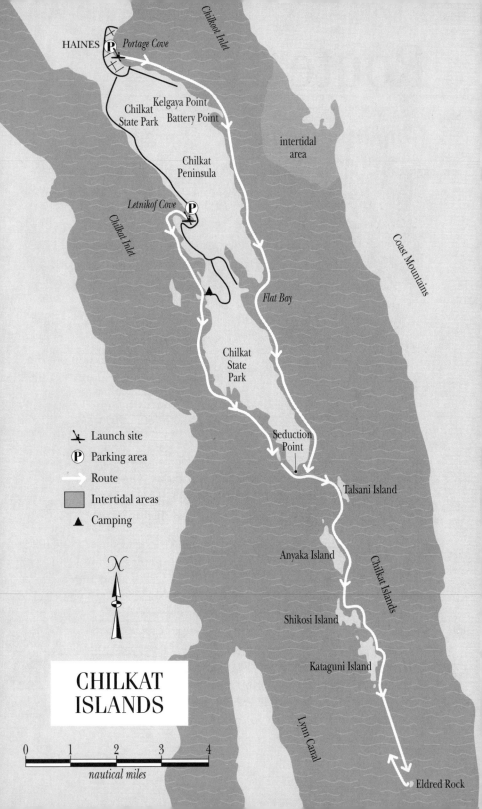

HAINES *Portage Cove*

Chilkoot Inlet

Kelgaya Point
Battery Point

Chilkat
State Park

Chilkat
Peninsula

intertidal
area

Letnikof Cove Ⓟ

Chilkat Inlet

Flat Bay

Coast Mountains

Chilkat
State
Park

Seduction
Point

Talsani Island

Anyaka Island

Chilkat Islands

Shikosi Island

Kataguni Island

Lynn Canal

⚓️ Launch site
Ⓟ Parking area
➜ Route
▬ Intertidal areas
▲ Camping

N

CHILKAT ISLANDS

0   1   2   3   4
nautical miles

Eldred Rock

winds pipe up toward midday, you will have accomplished most of the day's miles.

Be prepared for a longer trip if it proves necessary to wait out the wind. Or use a delivery or pick-up boat at the beginning or end of the trip.

LAUNCH SITE: Put in at Portage Cove on the east side of Chilkat Peninsula or at the small boat harbor in Letnikof Cove on the west side.

DIRECTIONS

Depending on launch site head south along east or west coast of Chilkat Peninsula. At **Seduction Point** begin island hopping south in Lynn Canal. Just how far you go on a particular day will depend largely on wind conditions and how much exploring you want to do. If you elect to continue all the way to **Eldred Rock**, be sure you have good weather— this is the longest and most weather dependent leg of the trip.

Where to Stay

CAMPING Camping is possible at Chilkat State Park and anywhere on the islands. There is no water available on the islands so bring along what you will need.

Route 19:

▬ ▬ ▬ ▬ ▬ ▬ ▬ ▬ ▬ ▬ ▬ ▬ ▬ ▬ ➤

Chilkat Peninsula—East

In settled weather, partial and full-day trips can be made spontaneously in this area, launching from Chilkat State Park or from Portage Cove in Haines. Overnight and longer adventures can also be planned. Views across and along Chilkoot Inlet are spectacular.

TRIP HIGHLIGHTS: Scenic views and observation of waterfowl and whales.

TRIP RATING:

Beginner/Intermediate: Day trips are suitable for beginners who are aware of the need to stop if winds and seas increase. More experienced paddlers will find this an easy and enjoyable paddle in settled conditions.

TRIP DURATION: Half day, full day, overnighters, or as much as three or four days if you go as far south as Seduction Point. The distance from Portage Cove to Flat Bay (also known as Mud Bay) is 6.5 miles. On to Seduction Point is another 4.5 miles.

NAVIGATION AIDS: NOAA chart 17317.

TIDAL INFORMATION: Plan the trip with flood and ebb tide in mind. Typical currents are not difficult to negotiate.

CAUTIONS: Watch out for increasing wind and accompanying rough seas. Chilkoot Inlet can be very rough at times. For this reason make your way along the shore and be prepared to stop and haul out if conditions deteriorate.

TRIP PLANNING: Before you set off get a current weather forecast. Plan your paddling for the early morning or in the evening. The long summer days often allow you the opportunity to break a trip into two parts with a haulout planned for the middle of the day when winds are more likely to be a factor.

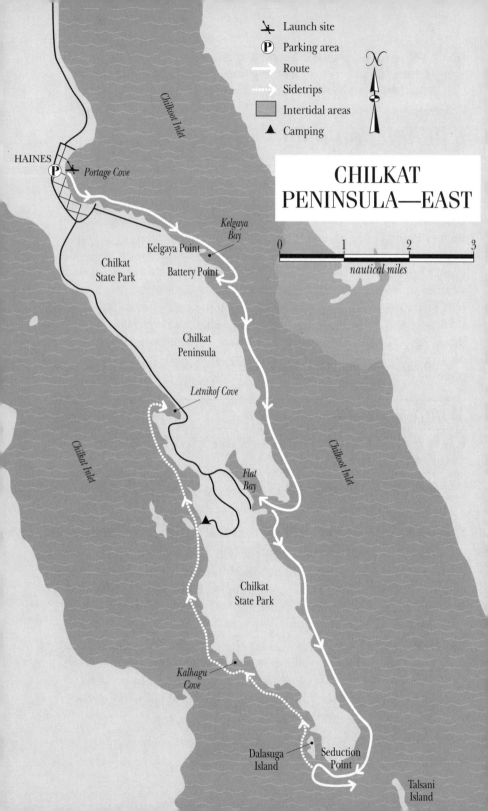

Launch site
Parking area
Route
Sidetrips
Intertidal areas
Camping

N

CHILKAT
PENINSULA—EAST

0   1   2   3
nautical miles

HAINES

Chilkoot Inlet

P ⊼ *Portage Cove*

Kelgaya Bay

Kelgaya Point

Battery Point

Chilkat
State Park

Chilkat
Peninsula

Letnikof Cove

Chilkat Inlet

Flat Bay

Chilkoot Inlet

Chilkat
State Park

Kalhagu Cove

Dalasuga
Island

Seduction
Point

Talsani
Island

LAUNCH SITE: Typically paddlers begin from Portage Cove in Haines. It is also convenient to launch from the shore of Chilkat State Park. Parking is available at both locations.

DIRECTIONS

From **Portage Cove** proceed in a generally southerly direction along the shoreline. For half-day or day trips a reasonable destination is **Kelgaya Bay**, which lies 2.5 miles south of Haines between **Kelgaya Point** and **Battery Point**. Farther along is **Flat (Mud) Bay**, which offers camping possibilities but does not provide good protection from south winds. From here on south it is 8.0 miles to **Seduction Point**. In the event bad weather should pin you down at Seduction Point, it may be best to wait it out. There is a hiking trail back north along the west side of Chilkat Peninsula, but it would be impossible to portage. *Sidetrips:* With two or three days available, it is possible to begin at Portage Cove and continue on around the peninsula to Letnikof Cove or to make the trip in the opposite direction.

Where to Stay

CAMPING   Camping is permitted at Chilkat State Park on Chilkat Peninsula or most any place along shore.

Glacier Bay & Gustavus

Those making their first visit to Glacier Bay National Park are easily confused about what is where. Here is a short explanation.

The headquarters for Glacier Bay National Park and all of the park facilities are located at Bartlett Cove. Gustavus (population 368) is the nearest *and only* town in the area; it is about 10 miles from Bartlett Cove.

To reach Glacier Bay it is necessary to either fly to Gustavus on Alaska Airlines from Juneau, take the Auk Nu ferry from Juneau, charter a floatplane to Bartlett Cove, or paddle to the bay on your own. The Auk Nu ferry does not take cars to Gustavus, but for an extra charge you can arrange to bring a kayak.

Once you arrive in Gustavus by air or water, it is necessary to use ground transportation to reach National Park headquarters at Bartlett Cove. The Glacier Bay Lodge bus meets all commercial airplanes and the ferry as does the TLC taxi *(phone 907–697–2239, e-mail: tlctaxi@hotmail.com)*. If you bring a kayak on the ferry, the taxi is your only land transport option. Those staying at a B&B in Gustavus can arrange to be picked up at the airport or ferry. If you are renting kayaks in Gustavus or at the park, ask about pickup service when you make your reservation.

Plan to arrive at Bartlett Cove with all of your camping equipment and supplies in hand. No supplies are available at Bartlett Cove except for white gas. There is one hardware store and one small grocery store in Gustavus, but transportation between Gustavus and the cove is expensive and sometimes slow.

The only designated hiking trails in Glacier Bay National Park are the day-hike trails at Bartlett Cove. However there is excellent hiking to be had in many places in the park where you can spend hours walking up the alluvial valleys fronting retreating glaciers.

Bartlett Cove

I t is logical to assume that you go to Glacier Bay to see glaciers. However it is important to realize that from park headquarters in Bartlett Cove, it is 35 miles to the nearest glacier. Others are as much as 55 miles distant. To actually see the gla-ciers, you can take a day cruise on an excursion boat, paddle a kayak for a few days, or plan a trip that combines paddling and the "up-bay" kayak transport service.

Although it is exciting to visit tidewater glaciers, there are other outstanding kayaking-camping locations in Glacier Bay that should not be missed. Because of the popularity of the glaciers, other places in the park offer more solitude and a more realistic wilderness con-tact. Some parts of the park are off-limits to all motor-ized vessels during the summer season. This means more solitude for you and that bird- and mammal watching will be excellent.

At Bartlett Cove there is a free National Park Service campground as well as Glacier Bay Lodge. The lodge has a dining room and hotel-type accommodations. It also offers a limited number of dormitory beds, a laundromat, and showers. There are several B&Bs in Gustavus. Kayak rentals are available in Gustavus and at Bartlett Cove. The cove is also the locale for day and evening guided kayak tours and the jumping-off place for week-long guided kayak-camping trips into Glacier Bay.

Kayakers going into Glacier Bay either begin their trips by paddling from Bartlett Cove, or they board a boat that will take them and their kayaks "up bay" to a designated drop-off point. The boat stops at specific points each day. You can get off at any one of them and be picked up at that location or at one of the oth-ers along the route at a later date. The exact number and location of pickup points varies from year to year. The points that I will note are based on those used in 1999, but there is no guarantee that they will be used when you arrive. There is one near the mouth of Muir

Inlet at Mt. Wright east of Garforth Island, which is convenient for those paddling the East Arm. Others are at York Creek, Rendu Inlet and Geikie Inlet.

The Park Service changes the drop-off/pickup locations frequently to avoid placing too much impact on any one spot. You can be sure that the transport service will be available, and you will be able to make arrangements with the transport concessioner at the Glacier Bay Lodge in Bartlett Cove on arrival.

Glacier Bay Quotas

Although the Park Service doesn't talk about it much, they are considering placing a yearly cap on the number of kayakers in the bay. So far the exact number has not been established nor has any kind of reservation system been outlined. However the possibility is in the offing. Hence it is a good idea to keep this in mind when making plans to paddle in Glacier Bay. (Park addresses for mail, phone, and e-mail are given in Appendix 5.)

There is a Park Service Visitor Information Station (VIS) at Bartlett Cove. All kayakers and campers must register here and attend a video orientation. Those kayaking-camping in the National Park are required to use the bear-resistant food storage canisters that are loaned free by the Park Service.

At the time of registering, it is important to find out which areas of the park are open to kayaking and camping and which are closed. Closures occur at places where birds are nesting, seals are giving birth, or kayakers and bears are not getting along compatibly.

Route 20:

━━ ━━ ━━ ━━ ━━ ━━ ━━ ━━ ━━ ━━ ━━ ━━ ➤

Bartlett Cove

Even though Bartlett Cove is the location of park headquarters, the lodge, and a boat mooring area, it is also a popular place for kayaking day trips. The cove generally offers protected paddling and opportunities to see humpback whales. It is also home to a variety of waterfowl. Occasionally black bears and moose are seen along the shore or even in the campground.

TRIP HIGHLIGHTS: Relaxed paddling and wildlife viewing.

TRIP RATING:
> *Beginner:* Unless there is much wind, this is an easy place for beginners to practice their skills while staying close to shore. Kayak rental companies give their orientations here as well.

TRIP DURATION: A few hours or one-half day's cruising. Bartlett Cove is 1 mile across and 2 miles long.

NAVIGATION AIDS: NOAA chart 17318.

TIDAL INFORMATION: Tidal currents are only significant at the head of the cove and these are easily avoided. Tide range in the bay however can be in excess of 20 feet, so when you haul out be sure your kayak is well up on the shore.

CAUTIONS: A variety of private and small commercial vessels move in and out of the cove. Occasionally floatplanes operate near the Park Service Dock. Stay near shore and leave the water if strong winds pick up.

TRIP PLANNING: No major planning is necessary.

LAUNCH SITE: It is easy to launch from the shore near the Visitor Information Station.

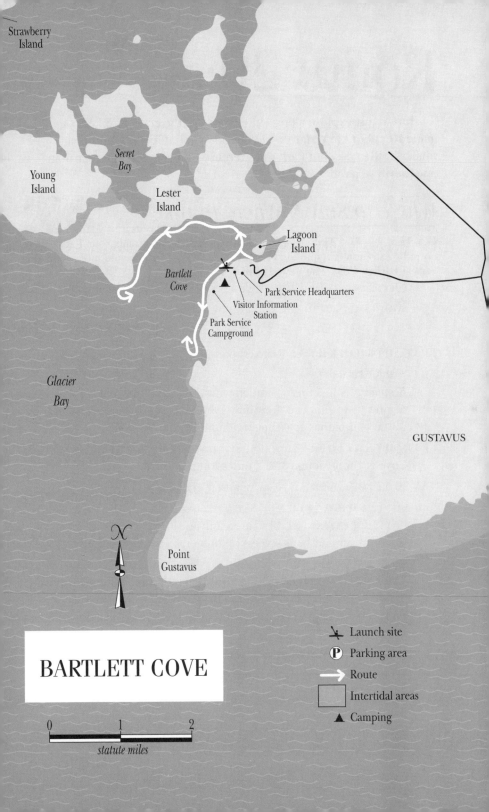

Strawberry
Island

Secret
Bay

Young
Island

Lester
Island

Lagoon
Island

*Bartlett
Cove*

Park Service Headquarters

Visitor Information
Station

Park Service
Campground

*Glacier
Bay*

GUSTAVUS

Point
Gustavus

N

BARTLETT COVE

Launch site

P Parking area

→ Route

Intertidal areas

▲ Camping

0   1   2
statute miles

DIRECTIONS

It is fun to just explore along either shore of the cove. Kayakers can maneuver about in order to have a good view of feeding humpback whales in the cove, but Park rules require that you get no closer than one-fourth of a mile.

Where to Stay & Where to Hike

CAMPING There is a free National Park Service campground at Bartlett Cove. Registration is required. **HIKING** There are several miles of hiking trails at Bartlett Cove. The VIS will give directions.

Route 21:

▬ ▬ ▬ ▬ ▬ ▬ ▬ ▬ ▬ ▬ ▬ ▬ ▬ ▬ ▬ ▬ ➡

Lester Island & Secret Bay

Lester Island provides the opportunity for a nice day trip or an overnight camping excursion that is close to Bartlett Cove and yet takes you into quiet and solitude very quickly. This is good bird-watching country, and along the shore you may see black bear and porcupine.

TRIP HIGHLIGHTS: Scenic peaceful paddling with the opportunity to see a lot of seabirds and land mammals.

TRIP RATING:

Beginner/Intermediate: Basic skills are required. You will be required to deal with some current and tide changes, but it is not a difficult paddle. It would be advisable for novice paddlers to be accompanied by an experienced person.

TRIP DURATION: The round-trip is between 10 and 12 miles and hence can be done in one day if you work the tides right. Otherwise consider camping for a night and returning to Bartlett Cove the next day. This trip could also be extended by continuing into the Beardslee Islands.

NAVIGATION AIDS: NOAA chart 17318.

TIDAL INFORMATION: It is necessary to plan this trip with the tides. You will leave and return to Bartlett Cove along the east side of Lester Island, an area easily negotiated near high slack water.

CAUTIONS: Avoid constricted passes between islands when current flow is high. Stay clear of the west side of Young Island where there can be very strong tidal currents.

TRIP PLANNING: For rounding Lester Island it is best to begin the trip about an hour before slack high tide. There is no water on the islands so bring along what you'll need.

LAUNCH SITE: Easy launching from the campground or the beach next to the Park Service dock.

DIRECTIONS

From the vicinity of the Park Service dock, head northeast to round **Lester Island**, continue northwest and then west to the **Secret Bay** entrance along the east side of **Young Island**. There is a portage—not a pass—between Lester Island and the unnamed island to the northwest.

Return to **Bartlett Cove** the way you came. It is also possible to return through the cut between Young and Lester Islands, but this is not recommended for most paddlers if there is any sort of south or southwest wind. The ebb and flood currents in this area can be difficult to negotiate at times. Leave this route to more experienced kayakers and the guided trips. *Sidetrips:* After exploring Secret Bay, paddle around in among the islands north of Lester Island. Just remember to get back to the pass into Bartlett Cove an hour or so before high tide slack.

Where to Stay

CAMPING   There is a National Park Service campground at Bartlett Cove.

Lester Island & Secret Bay

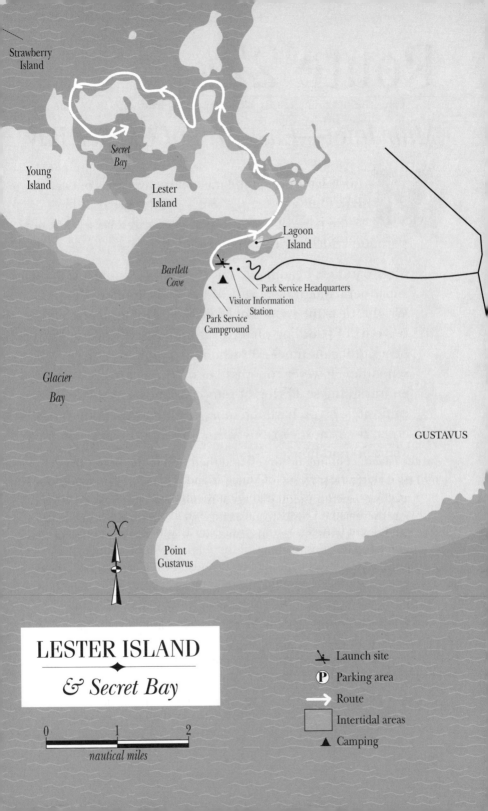

Strawberry
Island

Secret
Bay

Young
Island

Lester
Island

Bartlett
Cove

Lagoon
Island

Park Service Headquarters

Visitor Information
Station

Park Service
Campground

Glacier
Bay

GUSTAVUS

Point
Gustavus

N

LESTER ISLAND

& Secret Bay

⚓ Launch site

Ⓟ Parking area

→ Route

☐ Intertidal areas

▲ Camping

0   1   2
nautical miles

Route 22:

■■■ ■■ ■■ ■■■ ■■ ■■ ■■ ■■ ■ ■ ➡

Muir Inlet—East Arm of Glacier Bay

Muir Inlet is one of the most attractive parts of Glacier Bay. Only a few cruise ships visit this area, and in some parts of the East Arm, motorized vessels are not permitted during the summer months.

Most paddlers heading up bay do so by catching a ride on a camper-kayak transport boat to the drop-off at Mt. Wright, near the mouth of Muir Inlet. Doing so cuts about two days of paddling off a trip from Bartlett Cove and can be a significant time-saver when on a limited vacation schedule. However you miss out on the Beardslee Islands, an intriguing scattering of remote islands and solitude campsites. If you have the time, don't pass them up. They are at their most glorious with wildlife galore between mid-May and mid-June.

TRIP HIGHLIGHTS: On this trip you see the complete vegetation and geologic transition that accompanies glacial retreat. Along the way there is the possibility of seeing black and brown bears, seals, sea lions, wolves, moose, and an array of waterfowl as well as puffins and kittiwakes.

TRIP RATING:

Intermediate/Advanced: Relatively inexperienced kayakers will do fine if accompanied by an experienced companion or guide. Wilderness camping skills are as important as kayaking ability.

TRIP DURATION: A popular destination in the East Arm is McBride or Riggs or Glaciers. This is a round-trip distance of 74 miles from Bartlett Cove or between 35 and 40 miles round-trip from a kayak transport drop-off near the mouth of Muir Inlet. This is a minimum of six days for those who plan to be dropped off and picked up. It

includes one to two days paddle to McBride Glacier and an equal
amount of time to return, a couple of days in the vicinity of the
Glaciers, and one day allowance for any weather problems. Those
paddling from Bartlett Cove need ten to twelve days.

Sidetrips to Adams Inlet, Muir Glacier, or Wachusett Inlet add
additional days for some spectacular kayaking. Adams Inlet for
example deserves an additional two to four days, Muir Glacier an
additional one to two days, and likewise for Wachusett Inlet.

NAVIGATION AIDS: NOAA chart 17318.

TIDAL INFORMATION: Concern with tides applies to those who
elect to paddle from Bartlett Cove. It is necessary to pass behind
(to the east) of Lester Island on a flooding tide and to return on
an ebb well before low tide. In the Beardslee Islands ebb and flood
tides can significantly affect your progress between islands. Those
entering Adams Inlet are advised to do so on the flood near high
water and to leave on ebb shortly after high water.

CAUTIONS: Most important is to get off the water before wind and
wave conditions increase beyond your level of ability. Special care
must be taken when making any open-water crossings. It is possible
to stay near shore when paddling up the East Arm and most of the
way there are plenty of places to haul out to rest or camp. Those
who begin their trip at the mouth
of Muir Inlet need not cross
Muir Inlet. The
warnings mentioned

in the Paddling Southeast Alaska chapter regarding kayaking in the vicinity of glaciers applies especially to McBride Glacier. Furthermore the entrance to the small bay in front of McBride Glacier should be entered only at slack tide. Better yet, walk the shore and line your kayak until inside the entrance to avoid any difficult currents and renegade bergs that can come tumbling into the entrance.

TRIP PLANNING: Be sure you have everything you need before setting off. Once away from Bartlett Cove, there are no more services. A VHF radio is handy because the Park Service broadcasts a weather forecast twice daily.

LAUNCH SITE: Those paddling from Bartlett Cove can follow directions given for Route 21: Lester Island and Secret Bay. If you travel up bay on the camper and kayak transport boat, you will launch from a site somewhere near the mouth of Muir Inlet. The exact location of the launch point will change from time to time.

DIRECTIONS

When leaving from **Bartlett Cove**, paddle east to the head of the cove and pass **Lester Island** on a rising tide. This is much easier than trying to go out the inlet and north around Young Island. Tidal currents between **Young** and **Strawberry Islands** are very strong. Make your way north through the **Beardslee Islands**. There are many excellent campsites on these islands. Continuing north it is possible to paddle by **North** and **South Marble Islands** or stay farther east by way of **Leland Island** and **Sturgess Island** or along the shoreline. North and South Marble are rookeries and haul outs for sea lions, so just enjoy them from a distance of 100 yards or more. **Sandy Cove** is often closed to camping because of the number of bears in the area. Farther north follow along the **Muir Inlet** shoreline. Numerous campsite opportunities are available there.

Those who begin paddling from near the mouth of Muir Inlet will travel north along the east or west side of the inlet, depending on location of the drop-off. Because the transport drop-off service usually occurs in mid- to late morning, you will probably decide to camp one night at one of the many sites along the way to McBride or Riggs Glaciers.

Everyone seems to enjoy viewing **McBride Glacier** because of its ideal setting. The small bay in front of the glacier is a great place to paddle

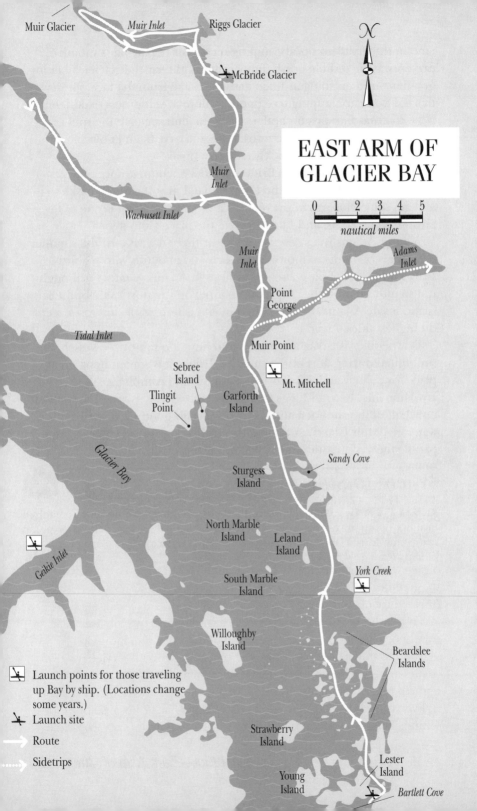

EAST ARM OF GLACIER BAY

Muir Glacier
Muir Inlet
Riggs Glacier
McBride Glacier
Muir Inlet
Wachusett Inlet
Muir Inlet
Adams Inlet
Point George
Muir Point
Tidal Inlet
Sebree Island
Mt. Mitchell
Tlingit Point
Garforth Island
Glacier Bay
Sandy Cove
Sturgess Island
Geikie Inlet
North Marble Island
Leland Island
York Creek
South Marble Island
Willoughby Island
Beardslee Islands
Strawberry Island
Lester Island
Young Island
Bartlett Cove

0 1 2 3 4 5
nautical miles

Launch points for those traveling up Bay by ship. (Locations change some years.)
Launch site
Route
Sidetrips

among icebergs and seals. Camping on the spit at the bay's mouth presents an incredible opportunity to see and hear the glacier moaning, groaning, and crashing as huge slabs of ice fall from the face. However this is a popular camping spot and is seldom a "wilderness experience." Note too that the spits on both sides of the entrance are the sites of struggling colonies of Arctic terns. Campers have been known to carelessly destroy their nests. Give them a break.

Instead of camping at McBride, consider spending more time just north at **Riggs Glacier**. It is no longer tidal, but you can still kayak to it and get some close-up impressions. The vicinity of Riggs is one of my favorite camp spots, and I usually have the place all to myself.

Sidetrip: Adams Inlet deserves a two- or three-day visit. In the summer the area is off-limits to motorized vessels and abounds with seabirds, seals, and moose. I have also seen wolves in Adams. *Caution:* Although not so indicated on the maps, the channel on the north side of the large island inside Adams Inlet has silted in and is impossible to cross except on highest tides. Avoid it.

Few people visit Wachusett Inlet and here too motorized vessels are prohibited during part of the summer. Hence it is sometimes a great place for privacy and remote-area kayaking and camping.

Up Muir Inlet beyond Riggs Glacier motorized vessels are permitted for only half of the summer, and it is an especially good place for bird watching. Muir Glacier is sometimes partly tidal, and so you can often paddle most of the way and walk partway for a visit.

Where to Stay

CAMPING   Once you leave Bartlett Cove, there are no more organized facilities of any sort. This is all undeveloped National Park wilderness area and except for specific spots designated by the Park Service rangers, camping is permitted anywhere you wish.

Route 23:

━━ ━━ ━━ ━━ ━━ ━━ ━━ ━━ ━━ ━━ ➤

West Arm of Glacier Bay

In terms of touring, the West Arm is the most famous area of Glacier Bay. Especially popular destinations are Grand Pacific Glacier in Tarr Inlet, Johns Hopkins Glacier in the inlet of the same name, Lamplugh Glacier, and Reid Glacier in Reid Inlet.

TRIP HIGHLIGHTS: Impressive, scenic glaciers; vast glacial outwash fans; and steep fjord walls dominate the scene. Wildlife viewing—brown bears, mountain goats, sea lions, and lots of seals and seabirds—is often excellent.

TRIP RATING:
Beginner/Intermediate/Advanced: Depends on where you begin and end your trip. For example, paddling from Bartlett Cove or from the drop-off location at the mouth of Muir Inlet to the West Arm can be hard going in places due to winds coming down the bay. However if you choose to put in at other drop-off points and stay on the south side of Glacier Bay—for example, paddling to and from Geikie Inlet or on the north side from Rendu Inlet—a kayaker of only moderate experience should have no problems.

TRIP DURATION: At a minimum this trip will be four or five days, depending on where you get dropped off and picked up. Trips of two or even three weeks can easily be planned for those paddling all the way from Bartlett Cove. The round-trip distance from Bartlett Cove to Grand Pacific Glacier is about 120 miles.

NAVIGATION AIDS: NOAA chart 17318.

TIDAL INFORMATION: Tides are not a significant matter. Be careful however on days when a brisk breeze is blowing against the direction of tide flow. Big waves can build quickly. At times like that it is better to stay in camp.

CAUTIONS: When paddling near the tidal glaciers, remain clear of the glacier face and do not get too close to bergs and floating ice blocks (see page 31). Campers at some locations in the West Arm have had problems with bears in recent years so be sure to follow the advice of the park rangers as to where and how you camp. It is no fun to get caught out in the middle of Glacier Bay with a building wind. Early mornings are usually the best times to cross.

TRIP PLANNING: Johns Hopkins Inlet is often off-limits for part of the summer when seals are giving birth. Other times it is difficult to impossible to get very near the front of the Johns Hopkins Glacier due to the ice pack. Locations in Tarr Inlet and especially Reid Inlet are sometimes closed to camping because of bear problems. In spite of these drawbacks, the West Arm is a huge area that can absorb a lot of kayak-campers. Consequently you may find more solitude here than in the Muir Inlet. A VHF radio is a good companion to have along.

LAUNCH SITE: Bartlett Cove or one of the transport service drop-off points.

DIRECTIONS

CAUTION: When leaving from Bartlett Cove, you should not even consider a direct crossing of Glacier Bay due to the very strong currents in Sitakaday Narrows. Take my word for it, I have been there and it is no fun.

From **Bartlett Cove** paddle east and then northwest around Lester Island; head northwest and then north to **Flapjack Island** at the north end of the Beardslee Islands. From here you can head for **Johnson Cove** on the northeast corner of **Willoughby Island**. Reverse your route for the return trip across the bay. You want to head up bay on slack water before a flood tide. Returning down bay use slack water preceding the ebb. Either way should be attempted only in calm weather.

Continuing on from Willoughby Island or starting from a drop-off point in **Geikie Inlet**, proceed northwest along the south side of Glacier Bay to your desired destination. From Willoughby to Geikie to **Grand Pacific Glacier** in **Tarr Inlet** is over 40 miles. Most paddlers can expect to spend three to four days on this adventure.

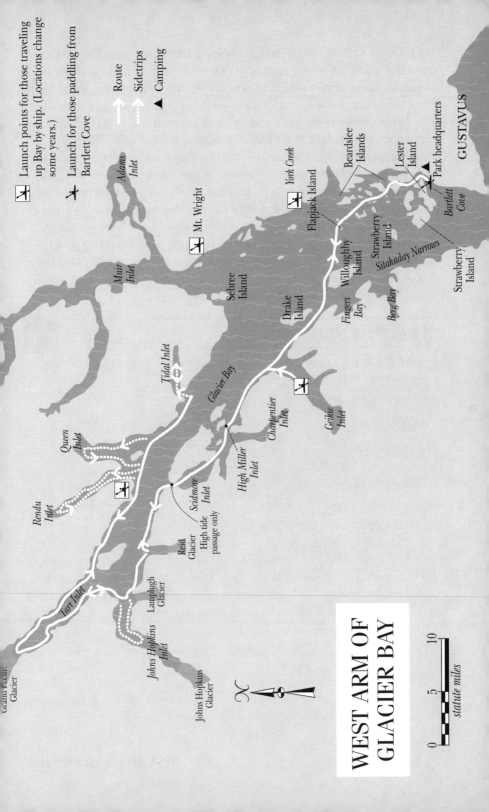

WEST ARM OF GLACIER BAY

statute miles

0 5 10

Launch points for those traveling up Bay by ship. (Locations change some years.)

Launch for those paddling from Bartlett Cove

Route

Sidetrips

▲ Camping

GUSTAVUS

Park headquarters

Lester Island

Bartlett Cove

Strawberry Island

Sitakaday Narrows

Strawberry Island

Beardslee Islands

Berg Bay

Willoughby Island

Fingers Bay

Flapjack Island

York Creek

Drake Island

Sebree Island

Geikie Inlet

Charpentier Inlet

Mt. Wright

Adams Inlet

Muir Inlet

High Miller Inlet

Seidmore Inlet

Tidal Inlet

Glacier Bay

Queen Inlet

Rendu Inlet

Reid Glacier
High tide passage only

Lamplugh Glacier

Johns Hopkins Inlet

Johns Hopkins Glacier

Tarr Inlet

Grand Pacific Glacier

For those starting from the Rendu Inlet area drop-off point, it is a matter of paddling along the north side of the bay. You will find some campsites along this route, but they can be scarce. There are some long stretches of sheer walls here. *Sidetrips:* When paddling along the north side of the bay, west of Sebree Island, you can make some fascinating excursions into Tidal Inlet, Queen Inlet, and Rendu Inlet. They all have receding glaciers, and this means you can find good campsites on their outwash fans, and there will be the numerous opportunities for hiking. And because few boats go there, you can expect some pleasant solitude.

Those transiting the south side of Glacier Bay on their way to and from the West Arm have numerous sidetrip diversions. Premier among them is Hugh Miller Inlet and areas to the west (discussed in Rte. 24). Geikie Inlet offers some great territory to explore. Fingers Bay and Berg Bay are choice areas to reconnoiter because they receive so few visitors. You'll find moose, bear, and lots of birds here.

Where to Stay

CAMPING   Other than areas specifically put off-limits by the Park rangers, you are free to camp anyplace.

Route 24:

━━ ━━ ━━ ━━ ━━ ━━ ━━ ━━ ━━ ━━ ━━ ━━ ━━ ━━ ➡

Hugh Miller Inlet & Environs

On the southwest side of the West Arm of Glacier Bay is one of the park's most scenic areas. There are no tidewater glaciers here, but there is great scenery— plus a lot of serenity and wildlife to watch, including bears, moose, and wolves. Scidmore Bay and Charpentier Inlet are off-limits to motorized boats in the summer time. You can take nice hikes up toward Hugh Miller and Scidmore Glaciers.

TRIP HIGHLIGHTS: Scenic views, solitude, wildlife viewing, and hiking.

TRIP RATING:

Beginner/Intermediate: Once inside Blue Mouse Cove or Hugh Miller Inlet, the paddling is generally well within the capabilities of novice paddlers. For those getting dropped off on the south shore of Glacier Bay, there is a minimum of alongshore travel to reach Hugh Miller. Those paddling from Bartlett Cove need to be experienced kayakers.

TRIP DURATION: Four days minimum if beginning from a drop-off point. The area deserves at least six days including travel time to and from one of the drop-off spots. Just paddling in Scidmore Bay, which is 5 miles long, and Charpentier Inlet, at 6.5 miles, can be a pleasant two- or three- day trip.

NAVIGATION AIDS: NOAA chart 17318.

TIDAL INFORMATION: Tides can be important in a couple of places: The passage from Blue Mouse Cove into the upper (north) end of Hugh Miller Inlet Bay is impassible at low tide because a spit has formed across here. Although it does not so appear on the NOAA chart or most topographic maps, it is possible to enter

Scidmore Bay from Glacier Bay on the north end of Gilbert
Peninsula on a high tide. This is a significant shortcut for those
traveling between Scidmore and the West Arm. The narrow tidal
channel into the basin at the base of Hugh Miller Glacial valley is
negotiable on high slack or low slack.

CAUTIONS: Crossings of Glacier Bay always require maximum care as
the wind and seas can spring up very quickly. Bears also deserve
constant caution.

TRIP PLANNING: Get the latest information from Park rangers on
what areas are closed to camping and kayaking. Bringing along a
VHF radio is a good idea.

LAUNCH SITE: Bartlett Cove or one of the kayak-camper drop-off
points.

DIRECTIONS

If you paddle here from Bartlett Cove, the suggestions for paddling
from Bartlett to the West Arm (Rte. 23) apply. The trip direction from
the drop-off point in Geikie Inlet is simply to follow the shoreline

Bears in Glacier Bay

Bears in the National Park are different from bears outside. Your attitude toward them and your game plan when dealing with them also needs to be different. Bears in Glacier Bay have picked up a couple of cognitive skills not possessed by their cousins outside the park. Because they are not hunted, they have less fear of humans, and because of careless campers, they know there is a relationship between free food and campsites.

You must keep your food in the bear-resistant containers at all times, keeping the containers closed any time you are not removing food or putting it back in them. Food preparation and cooking must be done low in the intertidal zone, well away from your tent.

When a bear in the park approaches your camp, you can be sure it is interested in food. If this happens and you are part of a group, everyone should stand together and make a lot of noise to discourage the bear from coming into the camp and destroying your gear. On the other hand, if you are alone or with one other person, be prepared at all times to pick up your cooking equipment and food and get it offshore in the kayak *quickly*. You do this for your safety and for the safety of all kayak-campers who will come after you. Once a bear learns that campers run away and leave food when it approaches, it is a done deal and no one is safe from then on.

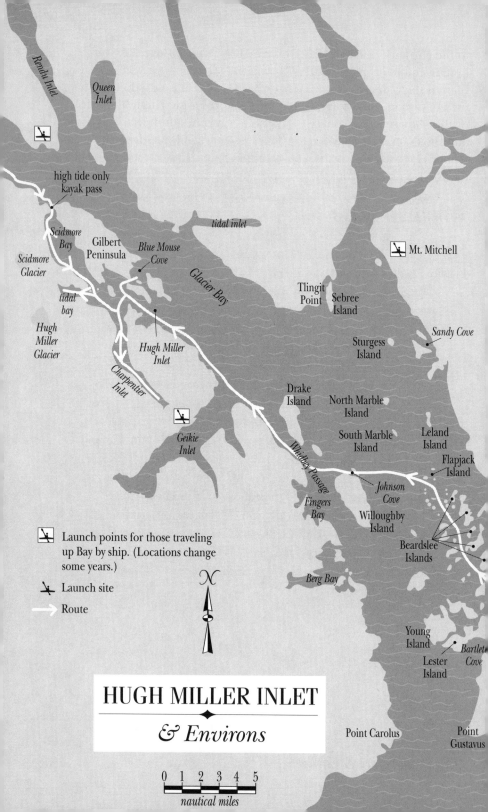

Renshu Inlet

Queen Inlet

high tide only kayak pass

tidal inlet

Scidmore Bay

Scidmore Glacier

Gilbert Peninsula

Blue Mouse Cove

Glacier Bay

tidal bay

Hugh Miller Glacier

Hugh Miller Inlet

Charpentier Inlet

Geikie Inlet

Mt. Mitchell

Tlingit Point

Sebree Island

Sturgess Island

Sandy Cove

Drake Island

North Marble Island

South Marble Island

Leland Island

Flapjack Island

Whidbey Passage

Johnson Cove

Fingers Bay

Willoughby Island

Beardslee Islands

Berg Bay

Young Island

Lester Island

Bartlett Cove

Launch points for those traveling up Bay by ship. (Locations change some years.)

Launch site

Route

N

Point Carolus

Point Gustavus

HUGH MILLER INLET

& Environs

0 1 2 3 4 5
nautical miles

to the entrance of **Hugh Miller Inlet** or **Blue Mouse Cove**. Reaching here from the drop-off point at Rendu Inlet is a bit more tricky because there is the wide expanse of Glacier Bay to cross. It is best done early in on a day when conditions are very calm. Once inside Hugh Miller Inlet or Blue Mouse Cove, you can make your way through the various islands and shoals, exploring as you go. The pass between Blue Mouse Cove and Upper Hugh Miller Inlet is a nice camping area. It is possible to make day-trip excursions from there into **Scidmore Bay** and **Charpentier Inlet**.

Where to Stay

CAMPING Check with Park rangers for any restrictions. Otherwise you can camp anywhere.

Hoonah
& Vicinity

Hoonah (population 900) is Southeast Alaska's largest Tlingit Indian village and the main community on Chichagof Island. It lies just inside Port Frederick. Because this is a no-frills working town of loggers and fishermen, it is off the tourist beat; cruise ships don't stop here. Consequently Port Frederick, just a four-hour ferry ride away from Juneau, offers tranquil remote kayaking.

Hoonah is a convenient starting place for kayak trips but not for outfitting or kayak rentals. However there are a couple of small food markets if you need a few more M&Ms to top off your trail mix. Hotels are at a minimum, but there are a couple of restaurants and ample camping spots nearby. Hot showers and a laundromat are available at the small boat harbor. Hoonah is visited by the Alaska Ferry Le Conte six times a week and connects with Juneau, Sitka, Tenakee Springs, Petersburg, Kake, and Angoon.

From Hoonah you can make day trips or take longer kayak-camping adventures. Kayakers come here because it is the starting place for the paddle cum portage to the hot spring at Tenakee Springs and to Southeast Alaska's primo whale-watching area at Point Adolphus.

Route 25:

▬ ▬ ▬ ▬ ▬ ▬ ▬ ▬ ▬ ▬ ▬ ▬ ▬ ▬ ▬ ➤

Port Frederick

Port Frederick offers generally calm and protected paddling. Forest clear-cutting detracts from some views, but the trade-off is the opportunity to view humpback whales, porpoises, seals, sea lions, and a variety of waterfowl in quiet waters close-up. Eagles diving for fish are a common sight, and it is an unusual day if you don't see a brown bear shuffling along the beach in more remote locations. Day trips from Hoonah can take you to the entrance of Neka Bay with a turnaround at Grassy Rock, Chimney Rock, or Midway Island. If you camp a few miles inside Port Frederick, there is ample time for exploring Neka Bay and adjacent North and South Bights—remote places you will likely have all to yourself.

TRIP HIGHLIGHTS: Viewing marine mammals, waterfowl, remote area camping, and solitude.

TRIP RATING:

Beginner/Intermediate: Basic kayaking skills are needed. By paddling near the shore, you will have plenty of opportunities to stop and haul out if conditions become troublesome.

TRIP DURATION: Part- or full-day trips (5 to 10 miles) can be made from Hoonah or from nearby camping spots. You can enjoy two- and three-day kayaking-camping trips in Port Frederick (20 to 30 miles round-trip). It is 17 miles from the vicinity of Hoonah to the head of Port Frederick.

NAVIGATION AIDS: NOAA chart 17302.

TIDAL INFORMATION: Paddling up and down Port Frederick will be a lot easier if you travel with the tidal flow. The only serious tide

Neka Bay Homesteaders

The last time I paddled up Neka Bay a highlight of the trip was visiting with Ed and Judy Wolf and their extended family who live far from the madding crowd. Their cabin in Neka Bay is obvious from the water, but chances are some member of the family will wave you over as you paddle by. In this part of the world, the occasional kayaker presents a welcome opportunity for conversation.

consideration is the salt chuck in Salt Lake Bay (discussed below in "Cautions").

CAUTIONS: In Hoonah Harbor there is a lot of fishing boat activity and frequent floatplane operations. Long Island, just south of Hoonah village, is a busy staging area for logging operations. There is a salt chuck at Salt Lake Bay in the upper reaches of Port Frederick. Rapids and strong currents occur here during flood and ebb. Only experienced kayakers should enter this pass on high water slack.

TRIP PLANNING: Consult a tide table. Watch for increasing winds and get off the water or stay near shore if whitecaps develop.

LAUNCH SITE: Most kayakers arrive in Hoonah on the ferry *Le Conte* as "walk-ons," carrying their kayaks and gear. Though not especially convenient you can launch from the north side of the Hoonah ferry terminal parking area at the base of the rip-rap slope. Kayakers with a vehicle can launch at the small boat harbor a mile south. There is no charge for launching or for parking at the marina. However if you leave a vehicle for more than the day, get some advice on where to park from the harbormaster or the Hoonah Police Department. *Caution:* Use care at the ferry terminal to avoid the wakes of passing boats while loading and preparing to get underway.

There is no specific route for paddling in Port Frederick. Each day will be different depending on when and where you start, the tides, and wind conditions. In the vicinity of **Hoonah**, stay clear of harbor activities. Fishing boats will be loading gear, off-loading fish, fueling, or heading in to and out of the boat harbor. But don't pass up this chance to observe the activities of a working, coastal Alaska village. Watch as huge halibut and hampers of salmon are hoisted up from fishing boats at the Hoonah Cold Storage.

Once clear of the harbor, proceed southwesterly along the south side of **Port Frederick**. Depending on your goals that day, you can closely parallel the irregular shoreline or simply paddle from headland to headland. After passing **Long Island**, the wilderness area begins, and immediately you are in the company of mergansers, harlequin ducks, eagles, and ravens. At rocky points and headlands, pigeon guillemots paddle about, dive, and carry food to their chicks in nests hidden in the rock crevices. In Port Frederick you will be accompanied now and then by feeding humpback whales. Their proximity is thrilling but not dangerous if you travel in shallow waters near shore. Porpoises and sea lions are likely to cruise by at any time. *Sidetrips:* Neka Bay and North and South Bights are excellent add-ons. Their crystal clear waters expose colorful sea stars, huge fluffy white sea anemones, and Dungeness crabs. You are sure to see single boar (male) brown bears or sows (mothers) with one or two cubs feeding on plants along the shore.

Where to Stay

CAMPING   No formal campgrounds exist in Hoonah. It might be possible to camp at the boat harbor, but it is not an especially desirable place. It is easier to paddle a short distance away from town and camp almost anywhere without problems. A convenient spot is Strawberry Island, which lies less than 1 mile south of Hoonah between Long Island and False Point. The easiest landing on Strawberry Island is the southeast corner. But bring water because there is none on the island. You can find numerous campsites within Port Frederick along the shore or on small islands, such as Chimney Rock. Another option is to use the Forest Service cabin in Salt Lake Bay about 15 miles from Hoonah harbor (see Appendix 2).

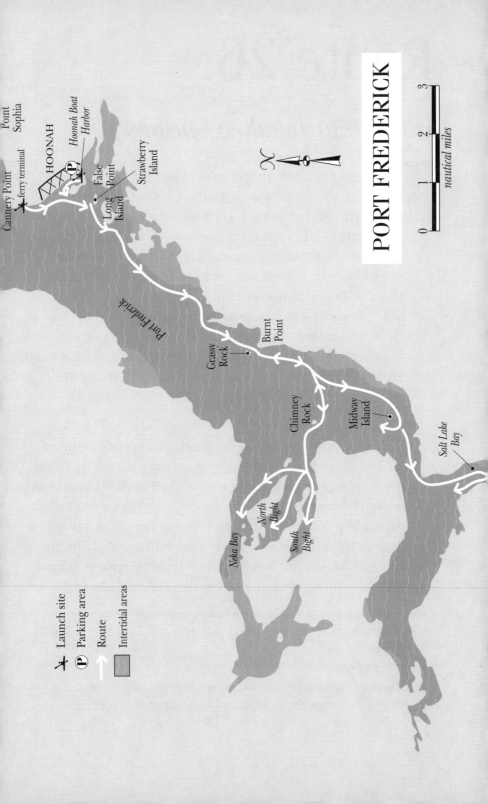

PORT FREDERICK

Cannery Point

Point Sophia

ferry terminal

HOONAH

Hoonah Boat Harbor

False Point

Long Island

Strawberry Island

Port Frederick

Grassy Rock

Burnt Point

Chimney Rock

Midway Island

Salt Lake Bay

Neka Bay

North Bight

South Bight

Launch site

Parking area

Route

Intertidal areas

0   1   2   3

nautical miles

Route 26:

▬ ▬ ▬ ▬ ▬ ▬ ▬ ▬ ▬ ▬ ▬ ▬ ▬ ▬ ▬ ▬ ▬ ➤

Hoonah to Tenakee Springs

This is a fascinating trip to the head of Port Frederick, where you make a short portage before continuing down Tenakee Inlet. It ends with the compelling option of soaking in a hot spring at the town of Tenakee Springs, a fascinating town with a population of 101. The ferry *Le Conte* stops here four times a week and will take you back to Hoonah or on to Juneau. Although this is a car ferry, there is no off-loading of cars in town. In fact there are no cars or roads in Tenakee. Amenities do include a post office, a library, a small grocery store, and a liquor store. There's also Rosie's Blue Moon Cafe, synonymous with Tenakee Springs, a gathering place for the town's eclectic and eccentric population.

This adventure in protected solitude is an opportunity to see lots of wildlife, including brown bears, deer, river otters, mink, humpback and killer whales, porpoises, seals, and sea lions. The time spent on this route can be short or long depending on the weather and your energy. It can be pleasantly extended with a variety of side- and add-on trips. In July and August the forest around Tenakee Springs is loaded with salmonberries, blueberries, and red huckleberries.

TRIP HIGHLIGHTS: Land and marine animal viewing, birding, wilderness camping, portaging, visits to a couple of unique Alaska villages, and a hot spring.

TRIP RATING:

Beginner/Intermediate: One or more members of this excursion should have experience in Alaska kayaking and remote camping.

Other members of the party can be of limited experience. It is a good trip for building paddling skills.

TRIP DURATION: Under ideal weather and tide conditions ambitious experienced paddlers can make this trip in two long days. To enjoy it more fully expand it to four or more days. The distance from Hoonah to Tenakee is about 42 miles.

NAVIGATION AIDS: NOAA chart 17302 combined with USGS *Sitka* at 1:250,000. NOAA chart 17300 offers less detail but is sufficient.

TIDAL INFORMATION: Proper timing is everything on this trip. Don't attempt the portage on a tide of less than 17 feet. Below that the approach to the portage point turns into a mud bog. Above 17 feet it is possible to paddle or line right up to the portage, an easy path only a few hundred feet long.

CAUTIONS: Tenakee Inlet has a long fetch and waves and white caps can build up in short order. Generally the north side of the inlet offers more protected paddling water.

TRIP PLANNING: Use tide table for best paddling and portage times. Trip scheduling includes fitting together the times for the ferry from Juneau to Hoonah, paddling to the portage to arrive at high tide, and then arriving at Tenakee Springs in time to connect with a ferry back to Juneau.

LAUNCH SITE: Same as launch site listed for Port Frederick (see Rte. 25). At Tenakee Springs plan to disembark on the beach next to the marina at the east end of town.

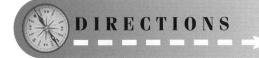

DIRECTIONS

Get underway as described for Port Frederick (Rte. 25). The most direct distance from **Hoonah** to the portage is about 17 miles. Under some circumstance, this could be done in one day. A couple of days is better. Take even longer if you want to do some exploring in the Neka Bay area. Getting to the portage requires paying attention to your map. The last 1.0 mile before the portage is a tidal creek that finally opens into a large slough. The portage trail is at the west end. There is no trail sign or marker, but the trail into Tenakee Inlet will be an obvious path.

From the portage to **Tenakee Springs** is about 25 miles. With the best tide and no wind or favorable light winds, a strong paddler can make

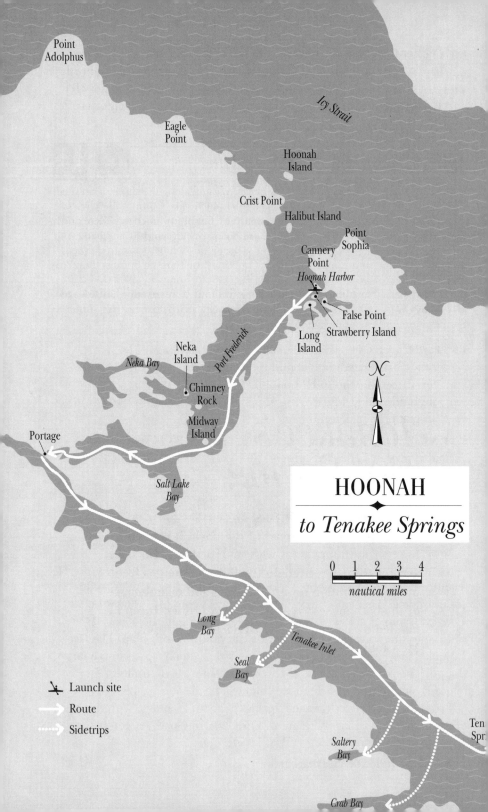

this in one day, but it will be more enjoyable to make it a two- or three-day trip. A significant seal colony lives on the small islands on the north shore of Tenakee Inlet. *Sidetrips:* Explore Long Bay, Seal Bay, Saltery Bay, and Crab Bay, all along the south side of Tenakee Inlet. Each is worth your time.

Where to Stay & Where to Hike

CAMPING   There are plenty of places to camp along the shore or on small islands in both Port Frederick and Tenakee Inlet. In Tenakee Springs there is a sort of campground "somewhere north of the marina," but pretty much anywhere north of the harbor is acceptable for pitching a tent. Keep a clean campsite and hang your food bags, there are a lot of bears around. During berry time bears are known to swagger down the town's main street with impunity. In Tenakee Springs there are limited cabins for rent from the Snyder Mercantile Company (907–736–2205), but don't expect anything to be available without a reservation in advance.

HIKING   Trails suitable for hiking run northwest and east from Tenakee Springs more or less paralleling the shoreline.

Tenakee's Hot Spring

The real pièce de résistance of Tenakee Springs is the bathhouse at the head of the dock. It is open twenty-four hours a day with specific hours for men and for women posted on the door. Bathing is free, but a contribution toward cleaning and maintenance of the bathhouse is reasonable and proper. It can be handed over to one of the clerks at the Snyder Mercantile Company across the road.

Route 27:

▬ ▬ ▬ ▬ ▬ ▬ ▬ ▬ ▬ ▬ ▬ ▬ ▬ ▬ ➡

Hoonah to Point Adolphus

The trip from Hoonah to Point Adolphus is not outstanding but the destination is. Point Adolphus is arguably the best place in Southeast Alaska to watch humpback whales. I don't think there is any summer day when you will fail to see several humpbacks feeding and cavorting in the nearshore waters. This is also the place to see a pod or two of sea lions, orcas, porpoise, and most anything else that comes in pods—except peas. An occasional sea otter will swim by, while eagles soar overhead.

There is excellent camping in Pinta Cove and on the west side of Point Adolphus.

TRIP HIGHLIGHTS: Watching humpbacks and other marine mammals at Point Adolphus.

TRIP RATING:

Intermediate: This is a simple paddle unless it is a windy day or especially unless wind and tide are opposed. If you paddle near the shore, it is easy to stop and haul out most anywhere. Kayakers with only minimal experience will enjoy it.

TRIP DURATION: Normally this is a six- to seven-hour trip covering a distance of 17 miles.

NAVIGATION AIDS: NOAA chart 17301.

TIDAL INFORMATION: It helps to have an ebb tide with you on the way to Point Adolphus, but even a flood tide can be managed.

CAUTIONS: In the vicinity of Point Adolphus, the longshore current combined with wind from the southwest can result in difficult but not dangerous paddling. Often by staying inside the kelp line you can make better progress. If winds and currents are unfriendly as you approach or begin to round Point Adolphus, there is good camping and whale watching from Pinta Cove.

TRIP PLANNING: Typically those making this trip arrive in Hoonah by ferry, not uncommonly in the middle of the night. Although seemingly inconvenient, remember the summer nights are very short, and you can easily get an early start from the terminal. Several times I have just thrown my sleeping bag down next to the terminal to wait a few hours for daylight and no one has objected.

LAUNCH SITE: Hoonah terminal. (See Launch Site information, Rte. 25.)

DIRECTIONS

Departing from the **Hoonah ferry terminal**, head northwest to **Cannery Point** and continue across Port Frederick Sound to pass north of **Halibut Island** and then on to **Crist Point**. Then continue on past **Flynn Cove** and **Eagle Point** to **Pinta Cove**. There is good camping at the cove. It is a good place to stop if the wind or sea is not to your liking. Otherwise continue on around **Point Adolphus** and find a campsite within the next mile.

Where to Stay

CAMPING There are broad shingle beaches backed by a forest and cliff at Point Adolphus. Numerous camping locations are available here. A couple of small streams supply water that should be treated.

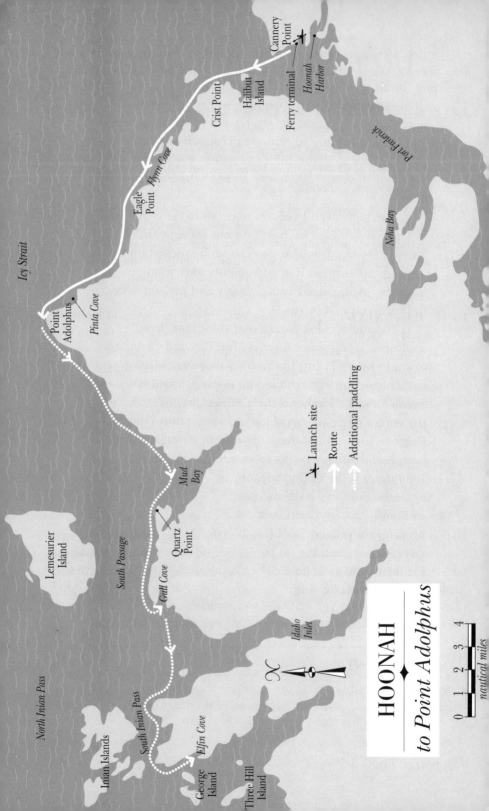

Cannery
Point

Ferry terminal

Hoonah
Harbor

Port Frederick

Neka Bay

Halibut
Island

Crist Point

Flynn Cove

Eagle
Point

Icy Strait

Point
Adolphus

Pinta Cove

Lemesurier
Island

South Passage

Mud
Bay

Quartz
Point

Gull Cove

North Inian Pass

Inian
Islands

South Inian Pass

Elfin Cove

George
Island

Three Hill
Island

Idaho Inlet

✈ Launch site

⇑ Route

⇑ Additional paddling

nautical miles

0   1   2   3   4

HOONAH
to Point Adolphus

After Point Adolphus

Point Adolphus is worthy of two or three days of watching whales from the beach and by kayak. After that the options are to return to Hoonah or continue on to Gull Cove in Idaho Inlet (14 miles), Elfin Cove (20 miles), or Pelican (37 miles), or even the big trip on to Sitka.

Very experienced kayakers may opt to cross Icy Strait to Gustavus or Glacier Bay. I do not recommend this 7-mile crossing. It is also possible to be picked up by a boat from Gustavus if arrangements were made in advance. (Appendix 1 lists delivery and pick-up services in Juneau and Gustavus.)

If continuing west from Point Adolphus, head southwest along shore toward Mud Bay and cross over toward Quartz Point. In this area there are often currents to contend with as you approach and enter South Passage. However their effects are mitigated to the extent that you stay close to shore. From Quartz Point to Idaho Inlet, there are usually extensive kelp beds and many sea otters to entertain you. At Idaho Inlet there is the option to stop at Gull Cove to visit the camp of South Passage Outfitters, head up into Idaho Inlet for camping, or continue on to Elfin Cove. (See Elfin Cove and Vicinity following for other trips.)

Elfin Cove
& Vicinity

Elfin Cove (population 50) is the one town in Southeast Alaska not served by any ferry. Scheduled floatplanes arrive daily, and it is possible to charter a flight from Juneau or Sitka. Kayak pickup and drop-off services from Juneau, Gustavus, and Pelican will also take you to or meet you at Elfin Cove.

The town of Elfin Cove is quaint and rapidly becoming "cute." There are no streets, just boardwalks around the two harbors, and everything is built on pilings. The cove is changing rapidly. A very few years ago, it was mostly a place where commercial fishermen came to off-load their catch. Today it has also become a collection of sportsfishing lodges and a place for the smaller cruise ships to visit. For kayakers it is a convenient place to begin, end, or stop by while paddling because there is a cafe, hot showers, coin laundry, post office, telephone, small grocery, and a liquor store.

There are virtually no kayak services in Elfin Cove, and accommodations there are mostly rather expensive package lodging-meals-fishing deals for fishermen. The best option for kayakers who want lodging in the Elfin Cove area is South Passage Out-fitters, which offers rental kayaks, pickup and drop-off services, laundry, and food and lodging options. At Hobbit

Hole in the Inian Islands, there is a B&B with kayaking rentals for customers. Kayak-campers find it convenient to camp at Granite Cove on George Island, just a couple of paddling miles north of Elfin Cove.

Area Currents

The currents around the Inian Islands are notorious. Velocities as high as eight to ten knots have been reported. Don't confuse North and South Inian Passes. Both can be difficult, but North Inian Pass is wider and much more challenging to cross. Unless you are a very experi-enced kayaker, it will be much better to catch a ride on a boat if it is necessary to cross North Inian Pass.

South Pass is narrower and easier to negotiate. Nevertheless absolute caution and respect for tidal currents must be exercised when transiting South Inian Pass around Point Lavinia . The easiest time to get around is during ebb and flood slack. If you plan to go through this pass, the local advice is to start about one hour before predicted slack. Choose a slack that precedes the current flow in the direction you want to go. For example, if traveling west plan to paddle through on high slack, and if heading east travel on low slack. Keep in mind that the waters in such places are never in fact completely slack. As you near Point Lavinia going west toward Elfin Cove, be prepared to encounter ocean swells. Cross Sound, which lies ahead, is open to the Pacific Ocean. Normally these swells are not a problem, but if unexpected they will quickly grab your attention.

Route 28:

Elfin Cove

Paddling in the cove, to the nearby islands, and into Port Althorp makes for some pleasant day trips in generally protected waters. The directions here are for those staying in Elfin Cove or camping on nearby George Island.

TRIP HIGHLIGHTS: This is a very scenic area with truly spectacular views of Brady Glacier in Taylor Bay. Sea otters and a variety of seabirds, including puffins, will keep you entertained as you paddle the ocean swells along spectacular granite cliffs.

TRIP RATING:

Intermediate: This is easy paddling that intermediate paddlers can enjoy as long as the wind is in their favor. In the vicinity of South Inian Pass and in channels around George Island, things become more challenging due to tidal currents, but these are easily avoided by planning your excursion with the tide tables.

TRIP DURATION: Half-day and full-day trips can be made, and of course they can be extended into overnighters. A lot of enjoyable day paddling can be done within 5 miles of the cove.

NAVIGATION AIDS: NOAA chart 17302 (with inset for Elfin Cove).

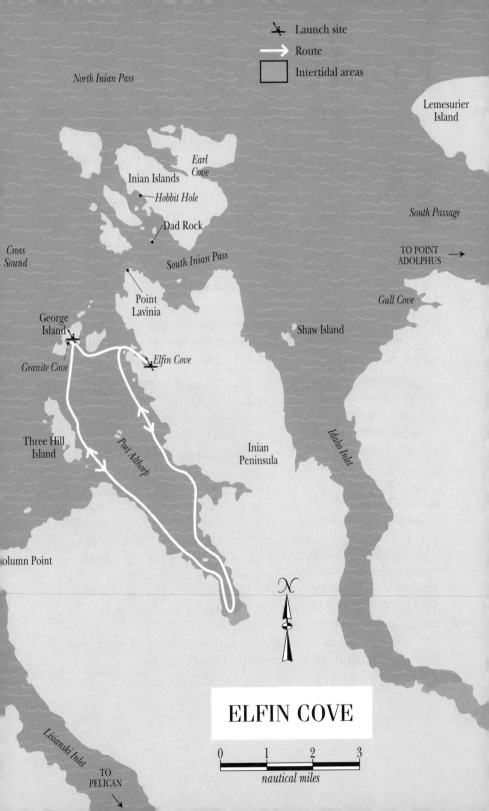

Launch site
Route
Intertidal areas

North Inian Pass

Lemesurier
Island

Earl
Cove

Inian Islands

Hobbit Hole

South Passage

Dad Rock

Cross
Sound

South Inian Pass

TO POINT
ADOLPHUS →

Point
Lavinia

Gull Cove

George
Island

Shaw Island

Granite Cove

Elfin Cove

Three Hill
Island

Port Althorp

Inian
Peninsula

Idaho Inlet

olumn Point

N

ELFIN COVE

Lisianski Inlet

0   1   2   3

TO
PELICAN

nautical miles

TIDAL INFORMATION: This is all deep water. Tidal currents are to be respected (see "Area Currents", on page 161).

CAUTIONS: (See discussion in "Area Currents.") In and near the Elfin Cove harbors, there is a lot of boat traffic by trollers and sports-fishing boats. These channels are narrow so give the boats the right of way by staying out of the middle of the channels. Floatplanes come and go throughout the day and always use the east entrance to the cove.

TRIP PLANNING: For day trips consider the weather forecast. For paddling in and around Elfin Cove (but outside South Inian Pass), the tide is to be reckoned with, but is not a significant control most of the time. For example, you can paddle from Elfin Cove to George Island most any time—you just may have to paddle a bit harder at times with a wind out of the west.

LAUNCH SITE: In Elfin Cove it is easy to launch from the numerous floating docks. In Granite Cove on George Island land on and launch from the beach with due respect for swells.

DIRECTIONS

In **Elfin Cove** you can paddle around in the two harbors without following any specific plan. *Caution:* The channel between the inner and outer harbor sometimes has a rapid tidal flow, especially on ebb. It is hard to get in any serious trouble here, but do watch for fishing boats and give them all the room they want and need.

For day trips out of Elfin Cove, you can exit by either the east or west entrance and then head west on the way to **George Island**, **Three Hill Island**, or to just paddle along the northeast side of **Port Althorp**. From **Granite Cove** at George Island, a paddle into Port Althorp or to Three Hill Island is a matter of heading south and southeast.

Route 29:

━ ━ ━ ━ ━ ━ ━ ━ ━ ━ ━ ━ ━ ━ ━ ━ ➤

Inian Islands

Exploring around and among the Inian Islands can make for a nice day trip or even an overnighter with camping on the islands. There are sure to be a lot of waterfowl in this area, along with sea lions, seals, and sea otters. Residents report there is one lonesome resident bear on the largest island.

TRIP HIGHLIGHTS: Exploring scenic coves and wildlife viewing.

TRIP RATING:
Intermediate/Experienced: Inexperienced kayakers should always go with an experienced guide, but once in the protected waters, such as Inian Cove, Earl Cove, and Hobbit Hole, they will have no problems.

TRIP DURATION: This can be a day trip from Hobbit Hole, Elfin Cove, or George Island or an overnight trip combined with camping on one of the Inian Islands. For example, a round-trip from George Island or Elfin Cove that goes around the Inian Islands represents 12 to 14 miles, offering opportunities to haul out in some of the islands' quiet bays.

NAVIGATION AIDS: NOAA chart 17302.

TIDAL INFORMATION: Paddling in the Inian Islands must be done with consideration of the tide-controlled currents previously mentioned. In addition to the potential difficulties in crossing South Inian Pass, the passes between the islands can be awesome.

CAUTIONS: Along with the warnings already given watch out for the "laundry," the local name given to a current-crazy channel on the east side of the southwestmost island. During flood race and ebb race, it is no place to be!

TRIP PLANNING: Obtain a weather forecast, consult the tide tables, and definitely plan your trip with care for the tide times. During maximum current flow, plan to be paddling in one of the quiet bays or haul out.

LAUNCH SITE: Elfin Cove or Granite Cove on George Island.

DIRECTIONS

From George Island or Elfin Cove, paddle north to **Point Lavinia**, then cross the South Inian Pass to the **Inian Islands** when tide conditions are appropriate. At or near slack tides, it is possible to travel between any of the Inian Islands. At other times it is interesting to explore **Inian Cove** or **Earl Cove** and paddle into the **Hobbit Hole** on a rising tide. When ready to head back to Elfin Cove or George Island, pick some slack or at least slow tidal flow and cross South Inian Pass by heading due south from Dad Rock. When across the Pass head west to Point Lavinia.

Where to Eat & Where to Stay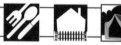

Meals and lodging are available at Hobbit Hole and in Gull Cove (see Appendix 1) if you make reservations in advance. This is not as formal as it sounds, but these are small places, and they need some advance notice so they can round up some fresh salmon or Dungeness crab for your dinner. In the summer there is usually a cafe in Elfin Cove.

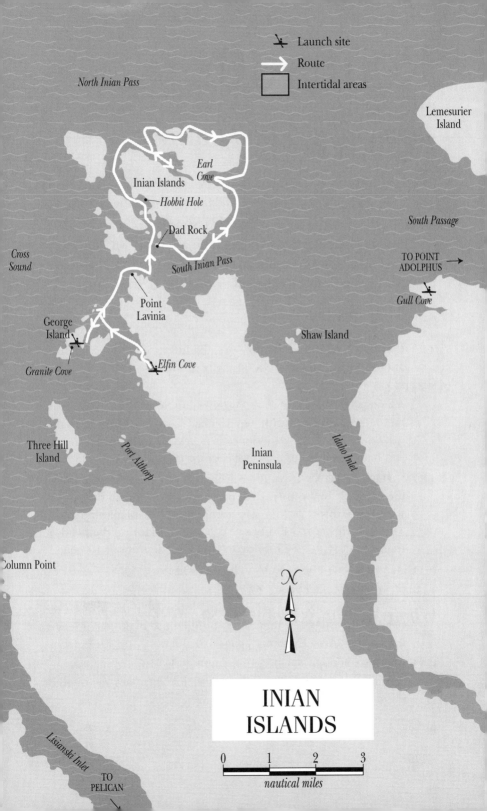

Launch site

Route

Intertidal areas

North Inian Pass

Lemesurier Island

Earl Cove

Inian Islands

Hobbit Hole

Dad Rock

South Passage

Cross Sound

South Inian Pass

TO POINT ADOLPHUS

Gull Cove

Point Lavinia

Shaw Island

George Island

Elfin Cove

Granite Cove

Three Hill Island

Port Althorp

Inian Peninsula

Idaho Inlet

Column Point

N

INIAN ISLANDS

Lisianski Inlet

TO PELICAN

0   1   2   3

nautical miles

Route 30:

━━ ━━ ━━ ━━ ━━ ━━ ━━ ━━ ━━ ━━ ━━ ━━ ━━ ━━ ━━ ━━ ➤

Idaho Inlet & Gull Cove

Idaho Inlet, a deep bay that extends 12 miles south from
South Passage, is "just around the corner" from Elfin Cove.
In this remote location you are sure to see a lot of sea
otters, Sitka black-tailed deer, and a few brown bears as you
paddle along shore. In July and August this is a great area
for pigging out on salmonberries, blueberries, and
huckleberries.

TRIP HIGHLIGHTS: Remote area paddling with lots of solitude
and opportunities to see a variety of animals.

TRIP RATING:

Intermediate/Advanced: Paddling through South Inian Pass should
be undertaken by or with experienced kayakers. Once in Idaho
Inlet only moderate experience is necessary with the proviso that
you haul out if winds and seas become difficult.

TRIP DURATION: If paddling from Elfin Cove or George Island,
the trip into Idaho Inlet is an overnighter, or one could easily
spend two, three, or four days camping in the inlet and exploring
with day trips. From Elfin Cove or George Island to the head of
Idaho Inlet is about 17 miles; to Gull Cove it is about 10 miles.

NAVIGATION AIDS: NOAA chart 17302.

TIDAL INFORMATION: Once in Idaho Inlet the tide can be used
to assist with travel up and down the inlet. Tidal flats exist at the
head of the inlet, but they are not difficult to negotiate. (See
sidebar on "Area Currents," page 161.)

CAUTIONS: Use great care when paddling in either direction
through South Inian Pass; plan your trips with slack near ebb or
flood depending on direction of travel.

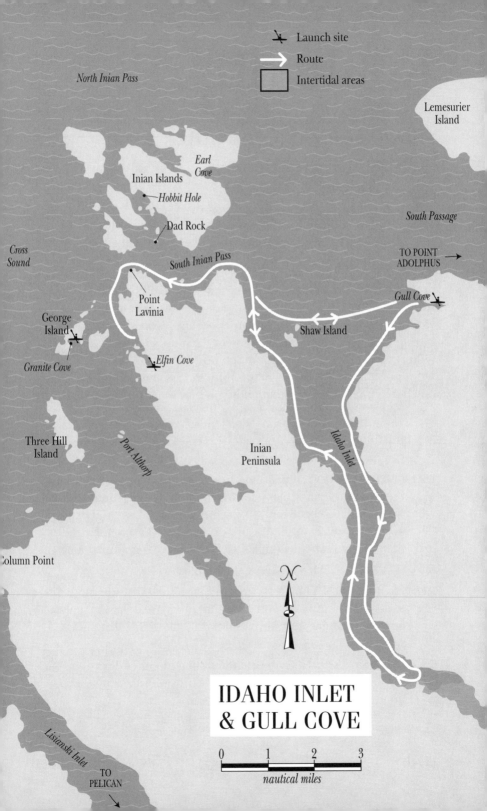

Launch site

Route

Intertidal areas

North Inian Pass

Lemesurier Island

Earl Cove

Inian Islands

Hobbit Hole

Dad Rock

South Passage

Cross Sound

South Inian Pass

TO POINT
ADOLPHUS

Point
Lavinia

Gull Cove

George
Island

Shaw Island

Granite Cove

Elfin Cove

Three Hill
Island

Port Althorp

Inian
Peninsula

Idaho Inlet

Column Point

𝒩

IDAHO INLET
& GULL COVE

Lisianski Inlet

TO
PELICAN

0   1   2   3

nautical miles

TRIP PLANNING: Obtain a weather forecast and consult tide tables for passage through South Inian Pass. Campers in Idaho Inlet are on their own, and in the upper reaches it not unusual to go days without seeing another person. Water is available, but you may want to bring your own supply.

LAUNCH SITE: George Island, Elfin Cove, or Gull Cove.

DIRECTIONS

Departing from the **Elfin Cove** area, travel north around **Point Lavinia** and then east through **South Inian Pass** on low slack preceding flood. Follow the south shore of the pass. Once in **Idaho Inlet** it will be easy to proceed along the west side. If departing from **Gull Cove**, to explore Idaho Inlet, paddle southward along the east shore of Idaho Inlet. Explore as you go and enjoy the quiet beauty. If you are just passing through the area, it may be convenient to camp on **Shaw Island**. Otherwise campsites can be found on both shores of the inlet. The mouth of Idaho Inlet between South Inian Pass and **South Passage** is as much as 5 miles wide. Consequently you may want to plan to make this crossing farther inside the inlet where it narrows.

Route 31:

▬ ▬ ▬ ▬ ▬ ▬ ▬ ▬ ▬ ▬ ▬ ▬ ➤

Dundas Bay

Dundas Bay is a special place that relatively few kayakers visit. Its upper reaches are definitely off the beaten track. It is part of Glacier Bay National Park, but since it lies 18 miles west of Bartlett Cove and only 6.5 miles north of Elfin Cove, it is described here. You are sure to see a lot of sea otters, river otters, black bears, deer, moose, and if you are lucky some wolves here. Ducks and geese are plentiful as well.

TRIP HIGHLIGHTS: Very scenic remote area with lots of waterfowl and wildlife, including a resident group of sea otters.

TRIP RATING:

Beginner/Intermediate/Advanced: Once well inside the bay, it is easy kayaking for any level of experience. The passage from Glacier Bay to Dundas Bay can include some strong currents, wind, and difficult seas under some conditions. It should be done by experienced paddlers. The crossing of North Inian Pass from the Inian Islands is definitely for very experienced paddlers *only*.

TRIP DURATION: It is worthwhile to spend at lest two or three days exploring, but there is enough fascination here for a week of paddling. A complete paddling tour of the bay is about 40 miles, but shorter trips are reasonable.

NAVIGATION AIDS: NOAA chart 17302.

TIDAL INFORMATION: There are some restricted channels in Dundas Bay that will be easier to explore when using the tide to assist you. In a few places there are small tidal flats. There are extensive intertidal sand flats at the mouth of the Dundas River and in the southwest part of the West Arm. If you go ashore in these areas, take precautions to not get stranded on an ebbing tide.

Crossing North Inian Pass

I encourage just about anyone new to Alaska kayaking to use a kayak delivery service to cross North Inian Pass the first time. The problem with this is that because Dundas Bay is part of Glacier Bay National Park, only a few boat operators are allowed to take kayakers there. To sort this situation out and to find a ride, talk to boat operators in Gustavus or get some advice from South Passage Outfitters (Gull Cove) in Idaho Inlet.

The major concern with tides however applies to paddling from Glacier Bay and especially crossing the North Inian Pass.

CAUTIONS: See "Crossing North Inian Pass" and "Getting to Dundas Bay" (page 175) sidebars.

TRIP PLANNING: No special recommendations for planning other than those given for currents. This is a remote area, and you will be on your own. There are several sources for water in the bay, but the Park Service urges that you filter or treat it. The most remote kayak-camping is in the West Arm of the bay.

LAUNCH SITE: Unless you use a drop-off and pickup boat to bring you to Dundas Bay, your original launch site may be Bartlett Cove, Hoonah, Elfin Cove, or even Pelican.

DIRECTIONS

Once inside Dundas Bay there are no specific directions to follow. The route shown on the map is one possibility, but you will want to break it up into two or three day trips. It is more a matter of exploring the inner

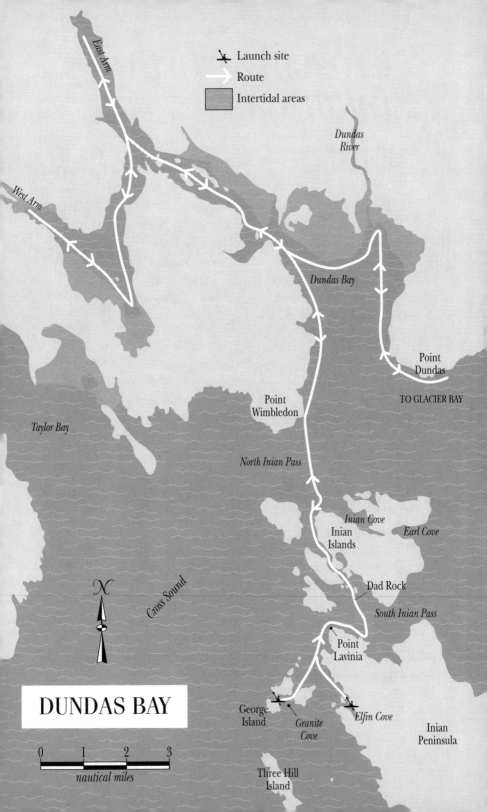

East Arm

West Arm

Launch site
Route
Intertidal areas

Dundas River

Dundas Bay

Point Dundas

TO GLACIER BAY

Point Wimbledon

Taylor Bay

North Inian Pass

Inian Cove

Inian Islands

Earl Cove

Dad Rock

South Inian Pass

Cross Sound

Point Lavinia

George Island

Granite Cove

Elfin Cove

Inian Peninsula

N

DUNDAS BAY

0   1   2   3
nautical miles

Three Hill Island

recesses of the bay as you see fit. There are more than 40 miles of shoreline to visit. An area often overlooked is the northeast corner of the main bay where the Dundas River enters the bay. Here the extensive tidal flats are fun to walk across in search of tracks made by wolves, bears, small mammals, otters, and waterfowl.

Getting to Dundas Bay from Glacier Bay

From Bartlett Cove it is a matter of crossing the bay to Point Carolus and then proceeding to Point Dundas (as shown on the map for Rte. 24). Experienced kayakers cross in a straight line from Bartlett to Carolus in very settled conditions, usually early in the morning. From there to Point Dundas, it is a matter of following the shore with some spectacular sheer rock walls along the way. Currents here can be strong, but even if they are running opposite your direction of travel, you may find back eddies to help you along.

Pelican
& Vicinity

Pelican is the epitome of a charming small village (population 149). It is a waterfront community built mostly on pilings. The main street is a boardwalk, and the closest things you will see to cars are three-wheeler ATVs. Most folks ride bicycles or walk. In years gone by a seafood processing plant was Pelican's raison d'etre, but each year its survival seems more and more in doubt. The town is searching for a new identity.

Tourists are not a significant part of the scene in Pelican. The town is too small to attract the big cruise ships, and when you stay around town for a day or two, everyone knows and welcomes you. There is a grocery store, post office, health clinic, three restaurants, hot showers, a laundromat, a B&B, and some now and then accommodations. If you are just paddling through Pelican or waiting for the ferry to come, camping is possible just outside the harbor on First Island.

To kayakers Pelican is an important jumping off place to explore the outer coast and visit such alluring attractions as Yakobi Island, White Sulphur Springs, Lisianski Inlet, Greentop Harbor, and Portlock Harbor. It is a nice stop on the way to Hoonah, Elfin Cove, or Sitka.

The AMHS ferry makes a round trip from Juneau to Pelican every other Sunday during the summer, and there are scheduled floatplane flights daily from Juneau and three times a week from Sitka. By planning a trip with the ferry schedule or with a combination of ferry and float-plane, you can arrange an excellent kayaking vacation.

There are now kayak rentals and kayak transport services in Pelican. The kayak pickup/drop-off option is worth considering. Pelican is the closest town to the several attractions of the outer coast, but it is still a long haul from town, down Lisianski Inlet to Lisianski Strait, and on to the ocean. Consider paddling out to the coast and then arranging a ride back from White Sulphur Springs or Greentop Harbor.

Paddling to the outer coast from Pelican can be serious kayaking. The beauty of the coast nearly defies description, but it is a remote place and winds and seas can pin you down for days. Before you leave Pelican make a point of leaving a floatplan with the harbormaster's office.

Route 32:

■ ■ ■ ■ ■ ■ ■ ■ ■ ■ ■ ■ ■ ■ ■ ■ ➡

Around Pelican

A number of half-day, full-day, and overnight trips can be made conveniently from Pelican Harbor. Just paddling along the waterfront and among the small islands in front of the harbor is enjoyable. With a little more time and energy, continue northwest past Pelican's "suburb" of Sunnyside and visit the Lisianski Inlet Wilderness Lodge. Day trips or overnighters also can be made by paddling southeast to the head of Lisianski Inlet 9 miles away.

TRIP HIGHLIGHTS: Scenic paddling.

TRIP RATING:

> *Beginner/Intermediate:* In the harbor area beginners will be able to hone their skills. Even traveling up or down the inlet is not difficult in settled weather. However the wind can create rough water when it comes rolling in from the west and northwest. At those times it is easy to find a convenient place to haul out along the shore.

TRIP DURATION: There are plenty of half- and full-day possibilities along shore for 5 miles in either direction or by crossing the inlet. A trip to or toward the head of Lisianski Inlet can be a long day trip, or better, extended into a pleasant camping excursion.

NAVIGATION AIDS: NOAA chart 17303.

TIDAL INFORMATION: Tide range in the summer is around 10 to 12 feet. Tide-driven currents are a factor in planning trips here as anywhere in Southeast Alaska, but they are not overwhelming. There are some intertidal areas near the head of the inlet, but they are clearly indicated on the NOAA chart.

CAUTIONS: Fog can be a factor on some summer mornings, but it need not affect your kayaking as long as you stay close to the shoreline. In Pelican Harbor be aware of floatplanes landing and taking off. Watch also for west winds that take over the inlet at

times. In Pelican the rule is that bright, clear, sunny mornings mean there will be strong westerly winds by noon—sometimes before noon—that will not calm down until 6:00 or 7:00 P.M. This wind can make for difficult paddling.

TRIP PLANNING: Obtain a current weather forecast before paddling, and keep the possibility of strong westerly winds in mind as you plan your day. If you do get caught out in rising west winds, be prepared to haul out, which you can do most places. Then if it is a typical day, it is a matter of waiting for a lull later in the afternoon or early evening.

Around Pelican   *-179-*

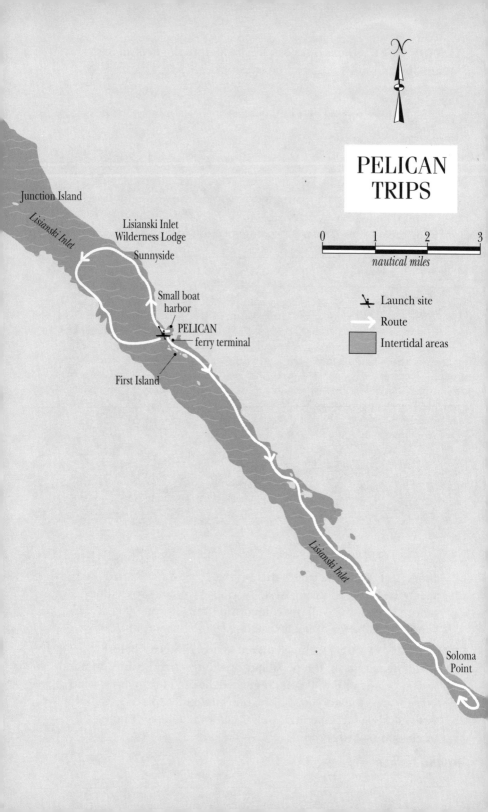

PELICAN
TRIPS

Junction Island

Lisianski Inlet

Lisianski Inlet
Wilderness Lodge

Sunnyside

Small boat
harbor

PELICAN

ferry terminal

First Island

Lisianski Inlet

Soloma
Point

0   1   2   3
nautical miles

Launch site

Route

Intertidal areas

N

LAUNCH SITE: Departures can be made from the Pelican ferry landing and from the small boat harbor.

DIRECTIONS

From **Pelican Harbor** head northwest or southeast, taking advantage of the tidal flow to help you along. Beyond that it is a matter of following the shore. If you feel comfortable with open water and the weather is fine, inexperienced paddlers can easily cross the inlet. I have found the eastern shore to be the most scenically fascinating for paddling up the inlet.

Where to Eat & Where to Stay

RESTAURANTS   In Pelican don't miss out on the excellent meals prepared by Karen and Victo at the **Lisianski Inlet Cafe** . Fresh fish, chowders, and seafood stews are the specialties. Karen is a pleasant Aleut with one of the warmest smiles in all of Alaska. She makes everyone feel comfortable and happy to be visiting Pelican. Catch her at a quiet time during the day and have a chat or ask her to play her accordion. **CAMPING**   Closest camping to town is First Island just outside the harbor. Otherwise you can camp most anywhere along the inlet. There are homes up and down the inlet from Pelican—select your campsites well away from them for your sake and theirs.

Route 33:

━ ━ ━ ━ ━ ━ ━ ━ ━ ━ ━ ━ ━ ➤

Stag Bay & Greentop Harbor

Stag Bay and Greentop Harbor are about 7 miles apart. Both are reached by paddling northwest in Lisianski Inlet, then southwest in Lisianski Strait. This scenic area is magic in the morning on still days when steep forested slopes are perfectly reflected on the glassy smooth waters of the strait.

Stag Bay off of Lisianski Strait is a quiet and peaceful body of water. There is nice camping on both sides of the entrance and possibilities farther up the bay. It is quite likely you will see brown bears in this area as you paddle along.

Greentop Harbor on the north side of Lisianski Strait is a fascinating and intriguing place. Rounding Point Theodore into Greentop Harbor is like entering a different world. There is a strange stillness in the air, and the waters are crystal clear. As you paddle along it is absorbing to look into the extensive kelp beds. The channels and islands in Greentop Harbor will keep you exploring for hours. A Forest Service cabin here is an original settlers cabin and definitely worth a visit. If the cabin is unoccupied, you are welcome to enter and look around. If someone is staying there, ask if they mind your taking a look at the historic structure.

TRIP HIGHLIGHTS: Remote and peaceful setting with plenty of opportunities for scenic views and wildlife.

TRIP RATING:

Beginner/Intermediate: Paddling within Lisianski Inlet or Strait, in Stag Bay, and inside Greentop Harbor can be handled by novice paddlers. However a good stiff breeze can sometimes blow up Lisianski Strait from the ocean; when it does it may tax the skills of a beginner.

More difficult and definitely requiring experience are the waters at the mouth of the strait and those as you turn into Greentop Harbor. (You are briefly paddling in the ocean.) Ability to handle swells and winds is essential. The safe way to do this is with a qualified guide or experienced companion.

TRIP DURATION: From Pelican the round-trip to the head of Stag Bay is 26 miles and will make a nice two- or three-day exploration. Extending this excursion to include Greentop Harbor makes it a 40-mile round-trip needing five or six days for ease and comfort.

NAVIGATION AIDS: NOAA chart 17303.

TIDAL INFORMATION: Travel up and down Lisianski Strait with the tide's assistance. There is no shallow or intertidal areas to be concerned with.

CAUTIONS: Difficult conditions often exist at the seaward entrance to Lisianski Strait as a response to the interaction of wind, tide, waves, and ocean swell. Plan to enter the mouth of Lisianski Strait on the flood; use special care at the entrance during ebb when currents and wind can produce rough waters. Fishing boats (trollers) operate in this area. Use special care in the vicinity of Junction Island.

TRIP PLANNING: Obtain a long-range weather forecast before setting out and leave a float plan with the harbormaster in Pelican. Consult the tide tables for paddling near and through Lisianski Strait entrance. If you plan to go all the way to Greentop Harbor, consider breaking the trip into two parts and spending one night in Stag Bay on the way.

LAUNCH SITE: Pelican small boat harbor or ferry terminal.

Stag Bay & Greentop Harbor

From Pelican head northwest crossing **Lisianski Inlet**, then proceed 5 miles along the south shore past **Junction Island**. Round **Rocky Point** into **Lisianski Strait** and follow the east shore southward. **Stag Bay** is 5 miles ahead. There is good camping on both sides of the entrance to Stag Bay.

When you are ready to continue on to **Greentop Harbor**, proceed on either the east or west sides of the strait to the harbor's entrance. On calm days it is no problem to cross over to the west side at any point. If there is much wind or swell, it is best to cross over to the west soon after passing Stag Bay to avoid crossing at the mouth of the strait where conditions may be more lively.

At the entrance to Lisianski Strait, you can pass inside of the two entrance islands as you round **Point Theodore** and make your way into Greentop Harbor, using due caution to deal with any ocean swells.

Sidetrips: One of the most highly praised trips in Southeast Alaska is along the outer coast of Yakobi Island. This however is serious kayaking for serious and experienced kayakers. The way north from Point Theodore to Cross Sound is open ocean coast. Although there are numerous coves and bays in which to take shelter, the headlands are exposed to whatever the Pacific Ocean has to offer as it delivers wind, swell, and tide into Cross Sound. Anyone undertaking this adventure needs to have time and supplies to allow them to wait out perhaps several days of any unpleasant weather.

Where to Stay

CAMPING   There are numerous possibilities for camping in Stag Bay and Greentop Harbor. However if you or part of your party are getting tired on the way to Greentop, it is better to stop for the night in Stag Bay and get a fresh start in the morning. Campsites between Stag Bay and Esther Island are not as numerous. Also, there is a charming Forest Service cabin in Greentop Harbor (see Appendix 2).

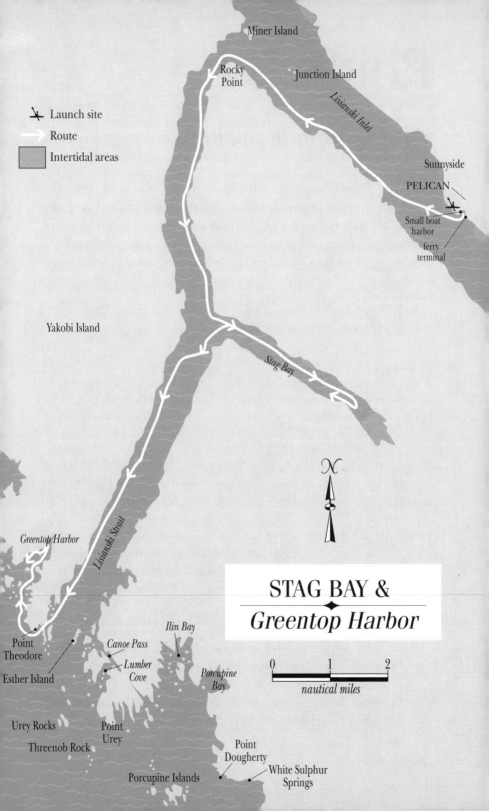

Miner Island

Rocky
Point

Junction Island

Lisianski Inlet

Sunnyside

PELICAN

Small boat
harbor

ferry
terminal

Yakobi Island

Stag Bay

Launch site

Route

Intertidal areas

N

Greentop Harbor

Lisianski Strait

STAG BAY &
Greentop Harbor

Point
Theodore

Esther Island

Ilin Bay

Canoe Pass

*Lumber
Cove*

*Porcupine
Bay*

0   1   2
nautical miles

Urey Rocks

Point
Urey

Threenob Rock

Point
Dougherty

White Sulphur
Springs

Porcupine Islands

Route 34:

White Sulphur Springs

White Sulphur Springs is one of Southeast Alaska's most popular destinations. On some days at the springs, you will be part of a motley assemblage of sailboaters, powerboaters, fishermen and fisherwomen, kayakers, and local residents from Pelican and Elfin Cove all soaking in the indoor and outdoor hot pools. The setting is scenic and the warm sulphur waters will rejuvenate even the most paddle-weary muscles.

TRIP HIGHLIGHTS: Soaking in hot spring waters, views of a scenic seascape, and an opportunity for ocean coastal paddling.

TRIP RATING:

Intermediate/Advanced: Those who paddle here on their own must be experienced and comfortable with open ocean shoreline conditions. There can be days when the sea is glass, but this can change rapidly to very difficult conditions even for experienced paddlers. Option: Take advantage of a drop-off and pickup boat service out of Pelican.

TRIP DURATION: White Sulphur Springs is about 20 miles from Pelican, and strong paddlers make the trip here in one day. Combine that with a visit of two days and the return makes it a four-day trip. Expand this with sidetrips to Green Top and Stag Bay going or coming.

NAVIGATION AIDS: NOAA chart 17303.

TIDAL INFORMATION: Tide range here is as much as 12 feet. Consider how tides can affect your progress up and down Lisianski Strait, especially when you enter or leave the mouth of the strait.

CAUTIONS: From the mouth of Lisianski Strait to White Sulphur Springs is 4.5 miles of ocean paddling. Swells can be significant.

Avoid the numerous rocks and islets along the way. The combination of wind, waves, and swell make for difficult paddling. Here navigation skills are important and a steering compass can help. Enter the mouth of Lisianski Strait on the flood and exit on the ebb with caution. In July and August trollers often operate near the mouth of Lisianski Strait; give them plenty of room to maneuver.

TRIP PLANNING: A good weather forecast is important to the trip. Plan you passages in and out of Lisianski Strait with the tide in your favor. If you are not an experienced paddler, either find an experienced companion, travel with a qualified guide, or hire a kayak transport boat to take you part of the way to or from the springs.

LAUNCH SITE: Pelican small boat harbor or ferry terminal.

DIRECTIONS

Proceed northwest to the mouth of **Lisianski Strait** (as described in Rte. 33). Paddle southwest around **Rocky Point**. Once past **Stag Bay** you will want to stay on the east side of Lisianski Strait and pass along the east side of **Esther Island**. On some charts it appears there is a protected shortcut available through **Canoe Pass** and **Lumber Cove**. Don't waste your time looking for it. Just continue out through the inlet, then take up a southeast heading to pass around **Point Urey**. **Threenob Rock** is a prominent and recognizable mark 1.5 miles ahead. Lay a course to pass just east of Threenob, and when it is slightly forward of your beam, pick up a more easterly heading to pass north of **Porcupine Island** toward **Point Dougherty**. **White Sulphur Springs** lies less than 1 mile beyond. Give a wide berth to the rocks along this route. They are obvious by breakers or disturbed water in their vicinity.

When you arrive at White Sulphur Springs, it's easy to recognize the site—there is a shelter over the hot spring and an adjacent Forest Service cabin. However landing a kayak right here is difficult to impossible under most conditions. The recommended landing is a small, somewhat obscured cove just west of the springs, which leads to a sand and gravel beach with campsites nearby. A short path leads from there to the springs.

White Sulphur Springs

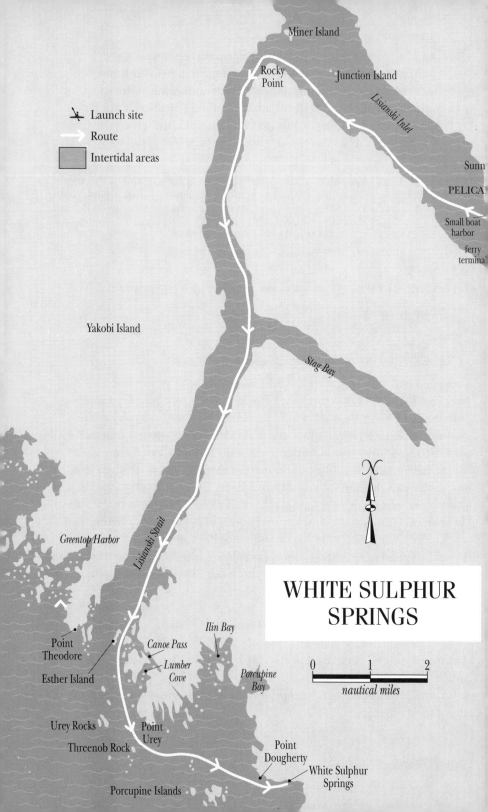

Launch site

Route

Intertidal areas

Miner Island

Rocky
Point

Junction Island

Lisianski Inlet

Sunn

PELICA

Small boat
harbor

ferry
termina

Yakobi Island

Stag Bay

N

Greentop Harbor

Lisianski Strait

WHITE SULPHUR
SPRINGS

0   1   2

nautical miles

Ilin Bay

Point
Theodore

Canoe Pass

*Lumber
Cove*

*Porcupine
Bay*

Esther Island

Urey Rocks

Point
Urey

Threenob Rock

Point
Dougherty

White Sulphur
Springs

Porcupine Islands

Sidetrips: The paddle to White Sulphur Springs is really just the beginning of numerous other fascinating trips. Just beyond White Sulphur Spring is Little Bay, a frequent hangout for gray whales. Continue on through scenic Dry Pass to Goulding Harbor, Pinta Bay, and Portlock Harbor (part of Rte. 41 between Sitka and Hoonah).

Where to Stay

CAMPING   There are a lot of places to camp between Pelican and White Sulphur Springs, but consider camping at Stag Bay on the way to or from Pelican (see Rte. 33). Also there is a much used Forest Service cabin at White Sulphur Springs (see Appendix 2).

Route 35:

━ ━ ━ ━ ━ ━ ━ ━ ━ ━ ━ ━ ━ ━ ━ ➤

Pelican to Elfin Cove

Pelican to Elfin Cove can be a trip of its own or a connector trip on the route between Sitka and Hoonah. It is a very scenic paddle when traveled from south to north. As you emerge from Lisianski Inlet into Cross Sound, you will be overwhelmed by a view of majestic snowy peaks of the Fairweather Range.

TRIP HIGHLIGHTS: Scenic paddling and good bird watching. Whales are often in Lisianski Inlet and Cross Sound.

TRIP RATING:

Intermediate: On days of settled weather, travel in Lisianski Inlet is easy enough. When it is windy it is no fun and no place to be if you are inexperienced. It is better to just camp and wait. The section from Column Point to Three Hill Island is in the exposed waters of Cross Sound. If things are rough, the less experienced paddlers are advised to wait for better conditions.

TRIP DURATION: Generally made as a one-day trip over a distance of about 19 miles. It can be made into two days if necessary.

NAVIGATION AIDS: NOAA chart 17302.

TIDAL INFORMATION: Use the tide to help you up or down the inlet. It is almost all deep water and there are no significant shallows.

CAUTIONS: Windy conditions in the strait can be a problem, especially midday west winds, as can swells in the Cross Sound part of the trip.

TRIP PLANNING: Use your tide tables and check the weather forecast. If you are setting off on a bright sunny morning, you can expect difficult wind out of the west by noon, which may force you to camp or wait until evening to complete your passage.

LAUNCH SITE: From Pelican via the small boat harbor or the ferry terminal. The reverse direction is from George Island or the harbor in Elfin Cove.

DIRECTIONS

Leaving from **Pelican** head northwest in **Lisianski Inlet** toward Cross Sound. At **Column Point** you can thread your way among the rocks if the weather is benign. Pass well inside of the green navigation marker as you turn northeast toward **Point Lucan**. With calm seas head toward the south end of **Three Hill Island** by way of the large rocky islet halfway there. This unnamed islet is the nesting place for puffins and black-legged kittiwakes. The puffins are often seen in the area flying in huge circles to check out visiting kayakers. Once you are in the lee of Three Hill Island, head north to **George Island** or northeast toward the entrance to **Elfin Cove**. *Sidetrips:* You can continue beyond Elfin Cove following Routes 27 and 30 and end up at the ferry terminal or boat harbor in Hoonah.

Where to Stay

CAMPING Numerous opportunities exist along Lisianski Inlet. Along the northern part of the inlet, the best campsites are on the west side. Farther on—but before the entrance to Lisianski Strait—there is better camping on the east side.

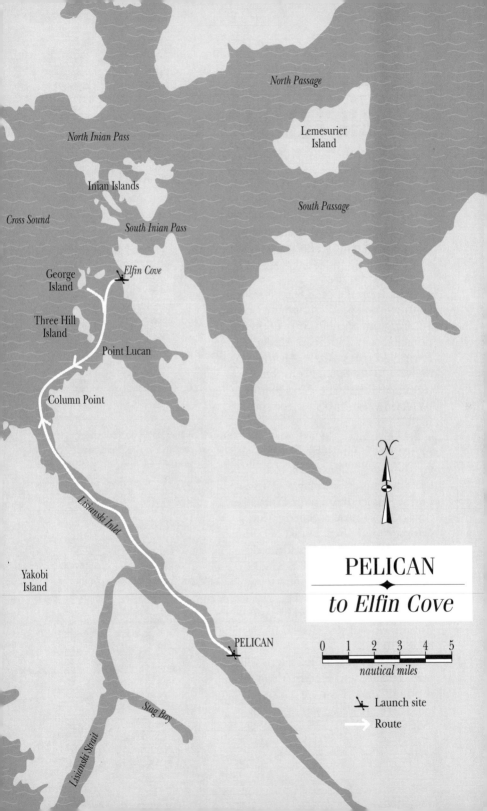

Sitka
& Vicinity

Sitka is Southeast Alaska's most historic city. Many consider it to be more beautifully situated than any of its sister cities. Nearby Sitka Sound is sprinkled with dozens of islands and coves that invite excellent kayaking.

Sitka (population 8,800) is served by the ferry from Bellingham, Washington, and has ferry connections to other Southeast Alaska towns and cities. Alaska Airlines has daily flights to Sitka. From there you can make floatplane connections to nearby towns or arrange for special flights to most any location.

In downtown Sitka there are hotels and restaurants as well as a youth hostel. Supermarkets and laundromats are available. The Forest Service has a visitor information center in town. Starrigavan Campground (U.S. Forest Service), one of Alaska's finest, is located near the ferry terminal. Several of the campsites are on the water, so you can easily come and go by kayak. The campground is 8 miles from town, but it is easy to hitchhike into Sitka.

Kayak services are excellent with sales, rentals, and pickup/drop-off shuttles. Guided trips are offered, and there are three sailing-kayak tours.

Route 36:

━━ ━━ ━━ ━━ ━━ ━━ ━━ ━━ ━━ ━━ ━━ ➤

Sitka Sound—South

In settled weather there is excellent paddling immediately adjacent to town. The numerous islands and coves between Middle Channel and Eastern Channel allow hours of rewarding and scenic exploration. On many summer days it is not difficult to visit still more coves and islands across Eastern Channel and make your way to Pirate Cove on Cape Burunof. Here you can picnic as part of a day trip or plan to camp overnight.

East of town beyond Entry Point, Eastern Channel leads into Silver Bay, a steep-walled fjord that extends nearly 6 scenic miles southeast.

TRIP HIGHLIGHTS: Opportunity to explore numerous small islands and coves. Bays and islands to the south of Eastern Channel offer more remote and peaceful paddling with the opportunity to see whales and a great variety of waterfowl.

TRIP RATING:
Beginner/Intermediate: In settled weather paddling among the islands of Middle Channel and Jamestown Bay is well suited to beginners. Those venturing farther afield should have more experience or be traveling with an experienced friend or guide.

TRIP DURATION: Excursions around Middle Channel and Jamestown Bay are all within a 2-mile radius of the Crescent Harbor launch site and well suited for a half-day or day-long schedule. Paddling into Silver Bay is an 8- to 10-mile round-trip and makes a nice day trip. If you continue across Eastern Channel to Aleutkina Bay and Cape Burunof, you will be paddling a total of 8 to 12 miles, an ambitious day trip or an overnight camping excursion.

NAVIGATION AIDS: NOAA chart 17326.

TIDAL INFORMATION: Tides in the Sitka area are significantly lower than elsewhere in Southeast Alaska, in the summer around 10 to 12 feet. Other than some thin water at low tide over tidal flats between Crescent Harbor and Jamestown Bay, the tide is of no great concern. Plan to go through narrow passes between islands and into bays on the east side of Eastern Channel at slack tide.

CAUTIONS: As with all commercial harbors, care is necessary to avoid encounters with powerboats. Cruise ships anchor between town and The Twins. On busy days there is a lot of boat traffic. All paddlers are advised to enter bays on the east side of Eastern Channel on or near slack tides to avoid difficult currents.

TRIP PLANNING: Consider the weather conditions and forecast before setting out. Throughout the area there are opportunities to stop and haul out on the lee side of most of the islands. Avoid landing near homes unless absolutely necessary. Carry binoculars and your camera in a waterproof bag. There will be a lot of photo opportunities as you paddle along.

LAUNCH SITE: Launch from the mooring floats in Crescent Harbor or from the ramp just inside the breakwater on the harbor's southwest corner.

DIRECTIONS

Leaving from **Crescent Harbor** head southwest across **Crescent Bay** to the islands south of **Middle Channel**. There you can meander around for hours among the numerous bays, islets, and rocks and still be within 2 miles of town. Waters near town offer protected paddling on most days. Those heading for the area south of **Eastern Channel** will be making a longer trip. They will either make their way through the Middle Channel islands or head down Crescent Bay to **The Twins** and from there continue south, southeast, or even southwest across Eastern Channel.

If **Silver Bay** or the upper part of Eastern Channel is your destination, exit Crescent Harbor and bear southeast along the shore and across **Jamestown Bay** on the way to **Entry Point**. *Farther along:* The foregoing area and trips can also be the stepping stones to numerous extended kayak-camping on south of **Cape Burunof** in the Necker Islands and beyond.

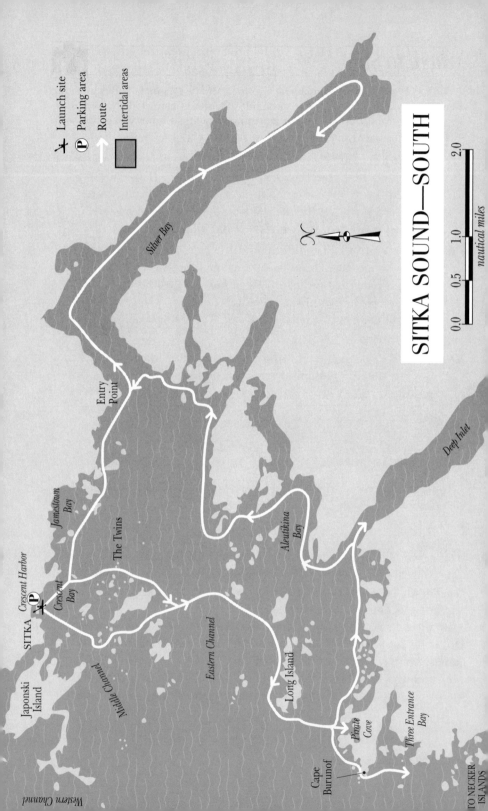

SITKA SOUND—SOUTH

nautical miles

0.0   0.5   1.0   2.0

Legend:
- ✈ Launch site
- Ⓟ Parking area
- ↑ Route
- ▢ Intertidal areas

Western Channel

Japonski Island

SITKA

Crescent Harbor

Ⓟ ✈

Crescent Bay

Jamestown Bay

Middle Channel

The Twins

Entry Point

Silver Bay

Eastern Channel

Aleutkina Bay

Deep Inlet

Long Island

Cape Burunof

Pirate Cove

Three Entrance Bay

TO NECKER ISLANDS

Where to Stay

CAMPING   Avoid camping near town in Middle Channel where a lot of the islands have private homes. On the south side of Eastern Channel, there are numerous places to camp. Water sources are unpredictable so bring along your own supply.

Route 37:

Sitka Sound—North

The islands north of Sitka Harbor offer fascinating opportunities for day trips and overnight camping. They can be easily reached from the harbor in Sitka or from the campground at Starrigavan Bay. A few of the islands have homes on them, but the local beauty is still intact. Views west toward Mt. Edgecumbe on Kruzof Island lend a spectacular backdrop on clear days.

TRIP HIGHLIGHTS: Scenic views and solitude easily accessible from town or from the campground. Waterfowl are abundantly present.

TRIP RATING:

Beginner/Intermediate: In settled weather kayakers with only limited experience can negotiate this group of islands. However the whole area is open to the southwest, and foul weather can develop quickly and unexpectedly. Beginners really should be accompanied by a knowledgeable guide or friend. Those of intermediate skills should have no problems if they are willing to haul out and wait for improving weather when necessary.

TRIP DURATION: Half-day, full day, and overnight excursions are all possible. The distance from Sitka Harbor to Big Gavanski Island and Starrigavan Bay is only 6.5 miles.

NAVIGATION AIDS: NOAA chart 17324.

TIDAL INFORMATION: Tides are of little significance here. In passes between islands tidal flow direction should be considered; it is always a good idea to paddle through them on slack water.

CAUTIONS: All the islands in North Sitka Sound are exposed on the south and west to the wind, waves, and swell of the Pacific Ocean. Kruzof Island to the west of Sitka offers some protection. You must be prepared to move into protected coves or haul out when an

adverse wind pipes up. Be aware of floatplanes landing and taking off in Sitka Channel. Be "heads up" for a variety of fishing and pleasure vessels that ply these waters.

TRIP PLANNING: Obtain a current weather forecast before heading to the islands. There are nice places to go ashore and have a picnic or camp if you plan an overnighter. Be sure and bring water for any trip. These small islands lack water sources. There are homes on some of the islands that should be avoided except in an emergency.

LAUNCH SITE: It is convenient to launch from the floating docks or from ramps at Crescent Harbor or Thomson Harbor in Sitka. There is also a ramp and plenty of shoreline for launching access near Starrigavan Campground.

DIRECTIONS

Make your kayaking plans in accordance with wind conditions and time available. When paddling here you are always near a place to haul out if necessary. Here are some route suggestions from typical departure points:

Departing from **Crescent Harbor** or **Thomson Harbor**, there are a couple of options. Proceed northwest and stay along the **Baranof Island** shoreline past **Watson Point** and cross over to **Kasiana Island** when it comes abeam. From there paddle along the east or west sides of **Middle Island.** An alternative is to follow the shore of **Japonski Island** and then island-hop toward **Chaichei Island** and up through the islands west of Middle Island. Leaving from **Starrigavan Bay** or its campground, it is convenient to head west to **Big Gavanski Island** and from there southwest on either side of Middle Island. These are all one-way trips of 6 miles or less.

Where to Stay

CAMPING Starrigavan Campground is a convenient place to set up camp for day-trip paddling. Away from town there are numerous pleasant camping spots on the small islands. Make an effort to choose a camping or picnic spot that is out of sight of houses.

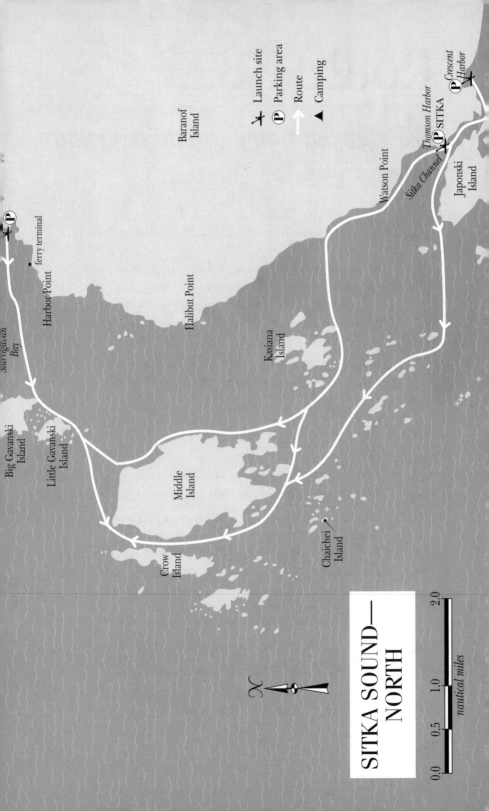

SITKA SOUND—
NORTH

0.0   0.5   1.0   2.0
nautical miles

Launch site
Parking area
Route
Camping

Baranof
Island

Watson Point

Thomson Harbor

Crescent
Harbor

SITKA

Silka Channel

Japonski
Island

Halibut Point

Harbor Point

ferry terminal

Starrigavan Bay

Big Gavanski
Island

Little Gavanski
Island

Middle
Island

Kasiana
Island

Crow
Island

Chaichei
Island

Route 38:

Starrigavan Campground & Vicinity

Any number of half-day and full-day trips can be made from the Starrigavan Campground or from the boat ramp nearby. Here a couple of them are suggested.

TRIP HIGHLIGHTS: Scenic locations, abundant waterfowl, and the opportunity to see a variety of mammals: river otters, deer, mink, and possibly bears. The creek that enters Starrigavan Bay is a salmon spawning stream and fishing is popular in the bay.

TRIP RATING:
Beginner: In settled weather all the trips here are easy to do. Newcomers to kayaking can get in a lot of safe practice while paddling along the shoreline of Starrigavan Bay near the campground.

TRIP DURATION: All are day trips within 6 miles of Starrigavan Campground.

NAVIGATION AIDS: NOAA chart 17324.

TIDAL INFORMATION: Tides not a significant factor.

CAUTIONS: Keep an eye out for sports-fishing boats and commercial boat traffic, including large ferry boats. Staying near shore as much as possible is the way for beginners to make this trip.

TRIP PLANNING: As always check the weather before you start paddling each day. Starrigavan Bay is normally protected water. You can go ashore nearly anywhere in this area as the land is either part of the campground or else is National Forest.

LAUNCH SITE: Starrigavan Campground or boat ramp. Parking is available at both places.

DIRECTIONS

The **Siginaka Islands** lie just 2.5 miles to the northwest of Starrigavan Campground and make for a nice part- or full-day paddle. Head first for **Lisianski Point**, less than 1.0 mile away, then paddle along the shore of **Lisianski Peninsula** until you reach a satisfactory crossover point to the Siginaka Islands. Here you can explore among more than

Starrigavan Campground & Vicinity

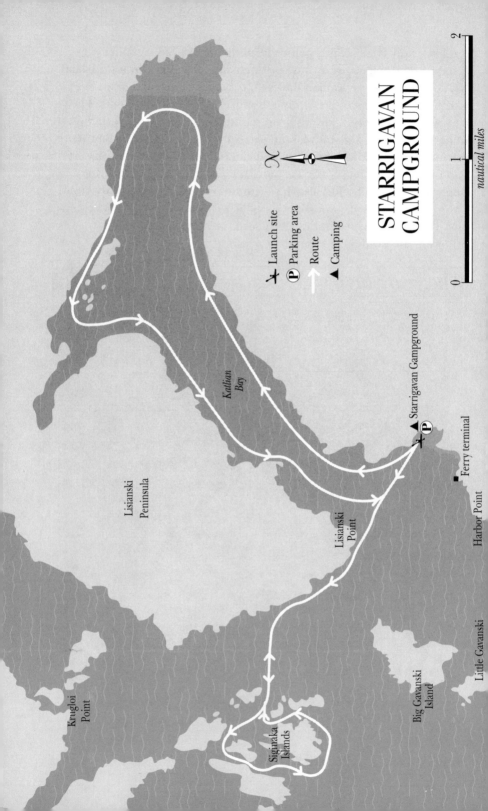

STARRIGAVAN CAMPGROUND

nautical miles

Launch site
Parking area
Route
Camping

Lisianski
Peninsula

Kalian
Bay

Lisianski
Point

Starrigavan Campground

Ferry terminal

Harbor Point

Krugloi
Point

Sigiraka
Islands

Big Garanski
Island

Little Garanski

0   1   2

ten large and small islands before heading back to Starrigavan Campground the way you came or by passing near **Big Gavanski Island**.

A quiet paddle up **Katlian Bay** is an easy trip from Starrigavan Campground. This round-trip is a distance of 9.0 miles and makes an easy day trip. On this route you can stay along the shore all of the way to and from the bay if you wish. In the central part of Katlian Bay, there are some small islands to visit, or you can haul out on the east or west end of the bay. *Sidetrips:* The locations and islands described in Route 37 for North Sitka Sound also apply to those kayaking from Starrigavan Campground. It is even possible to make a one-way trip to the Crescent and Thomson Harbors in Sitka by leaving from Starrigavan and following the Route 37 recommendations.

Where to Stay

CAMPING   Starrigavan Campground is ideally located. It is also possible to camp in the Siginaka Islands or in Katlian Bay.

Route 39:

![arrow]

Magoun Islands

The Magoun Islands lie in a beautiful remote area not very far from Starrigavan Campground or even from Sitka Harbor. Here you will enjoy a lot of small bays and islands that are well protected from most winds and seas. There is an opportunity to see a variety of waterfowl. Sitka black-tailed deer are abundant as are mink and river otter. If you are lucky you may see a brown bear or two.

TRIP HIGHLIGHTS: Remote area kayaking and camping a short distance from town.

TRIP RATING:
   Beginner/Intermediate: Novice paddlers should make most of the trip along shore rather than crossing open water. Once in the Magouns there is plenty of protection from wind and seas. However it is always necessary to pick the weather carefully when crossing the upper part of Sitka Sound.

TRIP DURATION: The round-trip distance between Starrigavan and the Magouns is about 16 miles, depending on the route chosen. An experienced strong paddler may want to make this as a day trip. It is better as a camping excursion of one or more nights.

NAVIGATION AIDS: NOAA chart 17324.

TIDAL INFORMATION: Some of the passes in the Magouns can only be negotiated on a very high tide, but there are enough options to allow you to bypass them.

CAUTIONS: Main concern is the possibility of a build up of winds and seas out of the southwest when paddling to or from the Magouns. Due care is also necessary for private and commercial boat traffic (see Rte. 38).

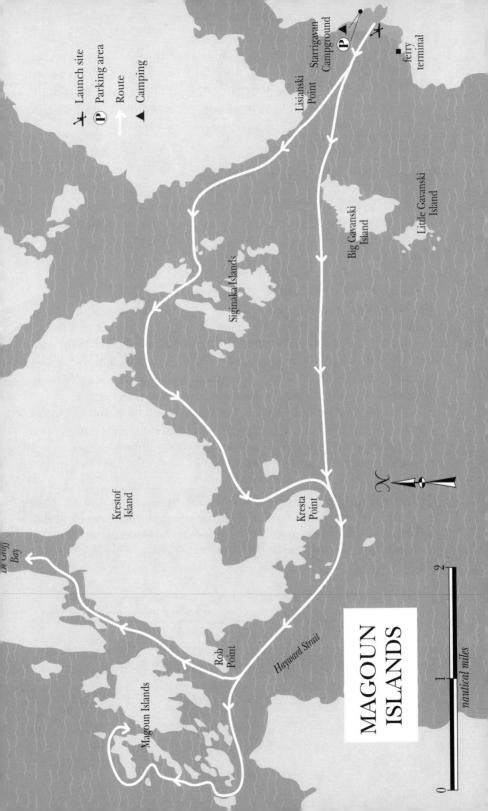

Launch site
Parking area
Route
Camping

Starrigavan Campground
Lisianski Point
ferry terminal
Little Gavanski Island
Big Gavanski Island
Siginaka Islands
Krestof Island
Kresta Point
De Groff Bay
Rob Point
Hayward Strait
Magoun Islands

MAGOUN ISLANDS

0   1   2
nautical miles

TRIP PLANNING: Obtain a current weather forecast and read the tide tables as you plan your adventure. Bring along plenty of water. It is scarce to absent in the summer. Begin your trip as early in the morning as possible to assure calm paddling conditions.

LAUNCH SITE: Starrigavan Campground or boat ramp.

DIRECTIONS

This excursion can be made by following the shoreline or using a direct route. Novice paddlers are encouraged to take the shoreline route at least on the trip out, going from Starrigavan to Lisianski Peninsula and then to and through the **Siginaka Islands** (described in Rte. 38). Continue on to **Krestof Island**, then follow around its south side to **Hayward Strait** and on into the Magoun Islands.

More experienced paddlers can take a more direct route west from Starrigavan to **Big Gavanski Island** and then direct to **Kresta Point** and into Hayward Strait. *Sidetrips:* Although I have never been there, an excursion into De Groff Bay on Krestof Island looks intriguing. Make it on a slack tide as there are a couple of narrow passes to negotiate. Another sidetrip combining hiking and kayaking is to Mud Bay, which lies due west of the north end of the Magoun Islands. *Farther along:* The Starrigavan to Magoun trip is also the beginning of the route to Salisbury Sound and beyond (see Rte. 41).

Where to Stay

CAMPING In the Magoun Islands and on the islands along the way, you can camp any suitable place. This is all National Forest land and open to visitors.

Route 40:

Nakwasina Passage & Sound

This is a pleasant overnight trip, although a very ambitious paddler may consider it as a challenging long-day paddle. It takes you into a remote area where there is usually plenty of wildlife and birds to keep you fascinated.

TRIP HIGHLIGHTS: Paddling in mostly quiet waters with scenic views and wildlife. Very likely to see bears cruising the shore in the early summer or visiting salmon spawning streams in July and August.

TRIP RATING:

Beginner/Intermediate: The portion of the trip in Nakwasina Passage and Sound is generally easy for relatively inexperienced paddlers. Olga Strait is always a busy place with boat traffic moving to and from Salisbury Sound. However you can avoid it if you desire.

TRIP DURATION: Day trip for a hardy paddler or overnight for a more leisurely approach. The total round-trip distance from Starrigavan Campground is 21 miles.

NAVIGATION AIDS: NOAA chart 17324.

TIDAL INFORMATION: There are extensive tidal flats (clearly shown on NOAA chart 17324) at the top of Nakwasina Sound, but they are not a problem unless you go ashore on a high tide and get stranded. Consult tide table for the passages on this trip, especially if you choose to paddle through Olga Strait.

CAUTIONS: If you include Olga Strait, watch out for boats and boat wakes in these restricted waters. Stay near the shore when paddling.

TRIP PLANNING: Obtain a current weather forecast to help determine the best way to paddle any forecast winds. You will usually experience protected paddling through Nakwasina Sound and Nakwasina Passage—as you find your way along either shore. Water is available locally, but it is best to take along what you will need for cooking and drinking. Excellent water is available at Starrigavan Campground.

LAUNCH SITE: Starrigavan Campground or boat ramp.

DIRECTIONS

From **Starrigavan Campground** bear northwest for less than 1 mile to **Lisianski Point**, then continue along the southwest side of Lisianski Peninsula to Dog Point at the entrance to **Nakwasina Sound**. Here you can decide to continue northwest into Olga Strait and on around **Halleck Island** by way of **Nakwasina Passage**. The other option is to turn northeast into Nakwasina Sound and follow Halleck Island around to Nakwasina Passage, then to Olga Strait. At that point it is possible to follow the Olga Strait southeast back to Starrigavan, retrace the route you just took, or make a much longer trip of it and enter **Krestof Sound**, returning via Magoun Islands (where you can pick up the way described in Rte. 39).

Where to Stay

CAMPING   No matter which route you take there are numerous opportunities for camping, including the islands in Nakwasina Passage. All of this area is National Forest and open to camping (see Appendix 2).

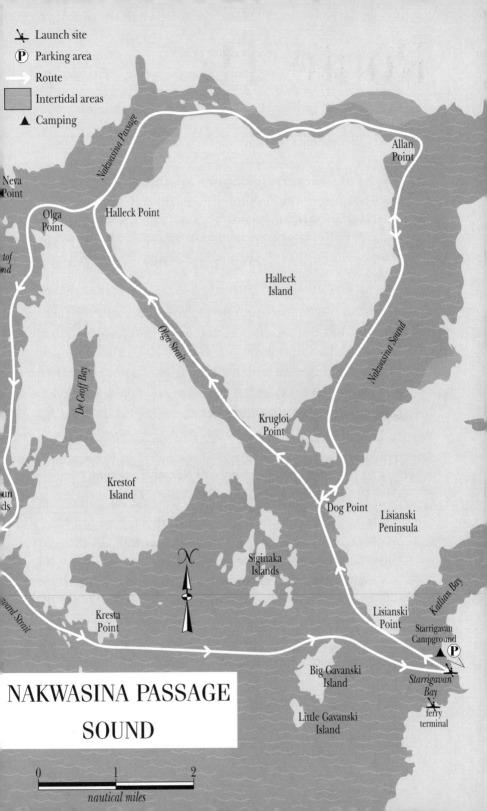

Legend

⚓ Launch site
Ⓟ Parking area
→ Route
▨ Intertidal areas
▲ Camping

Neva Point

Olga Point

Nakwasina Passage

Halleck Point

Halleck Island

Nakwasina Sound

Allan Point

...tof ...nd

De Groff Bay

Olga Strait

...un ...ds

Krestof Island

Krugloi Point

Dog Point

Lisianski Peninsula

Kaliian Bay

N

Siginaka Islands

Lisianski Point

Starrigavan Campground

...ward Strait

Kresta Point

Big Gavanski Island

Starrigavan Bay

Little Gavanski Island

ferry terminal

NAKWASINA PASSAGE
SOUND

0   1   2

nautical miles

Route 41:

━━ ━━ ━━ ━━ ━━ ━━ ━━ ━━ ━━ ━━ ━━ ━━ ━━ ➤

Sitka to Hoonah

Sitka to Hoonah is my favorite Southeast Alaska kayaking adventure. Although the whole trip is definitely designed for an experienced paddler, parts of it are in protected waters. Thus by utilizing a kayak delivery service from Sitka, Pelican, or Gustavus, several parts of this trip are within the abilities of nearly anyone.

This route takes you through a tremendous variety of coastal settings. You'll see every sort of marine and terrestrial mammal and a tremendous variety of waterfowl. The trip covers nearly 220 miles, including all sidetrip options. Sound like a lot of miles? It really isn't if you have and take the time to enjoy it. More aggressive paddlers who bypass the sidetrips are looking at a distance of only about 130 miles.

This trip can be run in either direction, starting in Hoonah or Sitka, or a part of it can be run, starting or ending in Pelican. The choices of Hoonah, Sitka, and Pelican reflect the fact that each town is on the AMHS ferry route. (Note that the ferry only visits Pelican twice a month.) Although this route does include some open ocean paddling, it does not include crossing any major sounds except Salisbury Sound, which can be easily skirted.

TRIP HIGHLIGHTS: Challenging trip through a variety of land- and seascapes; tremendous views and lot of opportunities to view a variety of wildlife.

TRIP RATING:
Beginner/Intermediate/Advanced: The whole trip is for experienced paddlers with a flexible schedule. Portions of the trip can be easily

handled by inexperienced kayakers if they utilize a drop-off and pickup service. As always beginners will benefit by traveling with an experienced paddler.

TRIP DURATION: To do this trip at an enjoyable pace with time for difficult weather, allow three weeks. I have made the trip twice— once in each direction and both times spent three weeks from start to finish. Strong, experienced paddlers following the most direct route could easily cover the distance of 130 miles in a week or less in good weather.

NAVIGATION AIDS: NOAA charts 17301, 17302, 17321, 17322, 17323, 17324.

TIDAL INFORMATION: Tide plays a role throughout the trip, making paddling easier by using tidal flow. In a variety of locations, such as Sukoi Inlet, Klag Bay, Lake Anna, Sister Lake, Dry Pass, and South Inian Pass, the tides will control the possibility of passage and/or make for dangerous conditions (see Directions following).

CAUTIONS: A portion of this trip is along the open ocean coast of Chichagof Island. Here great care must be exercised. In several places along the way you will be completely on your own and out of contact with anyone, even with a VHF radio because topographic variations affect reception and transmission. It is important to have proper camping equipment and apparel, a reliable first aid kit, and sufficient food.

TRIP PLANNING: Be sure all equipment is in its best condition. There are areas, such as around Khaz Bay and the Myriad Islands, where a steering compass will be helpful. Before beginning the trip leave a proposed float plan with someone and then make a point of calling them when phones are available and on arrival in Hoonah. Good judgement *must* be exercised regarding weather.

LAUNCH SITE: Initial put-in points include Starrigavan Bay in Sitka, the small boat harbor in Pelican, and the ferry terminal or small boat harbor in Hoonah.

DIRECTIONS

Departing from **Starrigavan Bay** head northwest and west for **Krestof Sound** (as described in Rte. 39). At the north end of Krestof Sound,

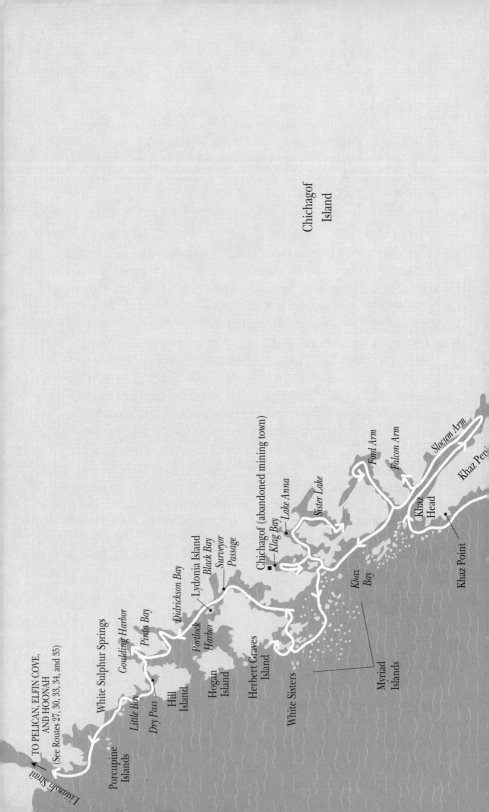

Chichagof Island

Chichagof (abandoned mining town)

Klag Bay
Lake Anna
Sister Lake

Fond Arm
Falcon Arm
Slocum Arm
Khaz Head
Khaz Peni

Khaz
Bay

Khaz Point

Myriad Islands

White Sisters

Herbert Graves Island

Portlock Harbor
Hogan Island

Black Bay
Lydonia Island
Surveyor Passage

Didrickson Bay

Hill Island

Pinta Bay

Goulding Harbor
White Sulphur Springs
Little Bay
Dry Pass

Porcupine Islands

TO PELICAN, ELFIN COVE,
AND HOONAH
(See Routes 27, 30, 33, 34, and 35)

Lisianski Strait

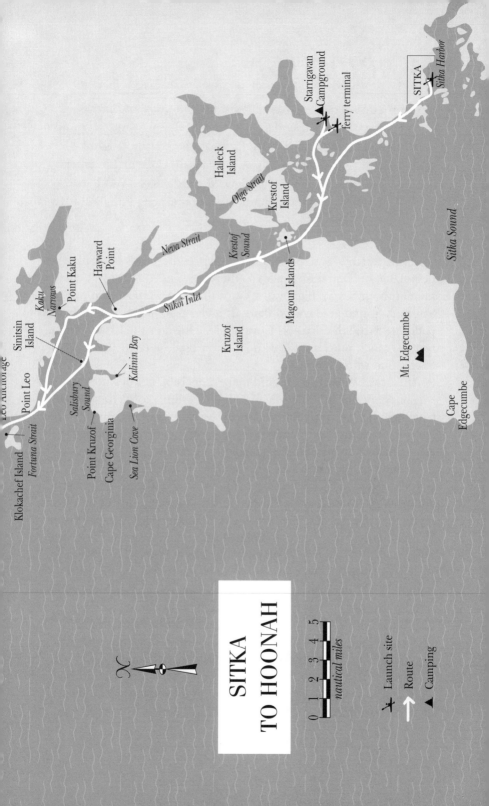

SITKA
TO HOONAH

0 1 2 3 4 5
nautical miles

✈ Launch site
⬆ Route
▲ Camping

SITKA
Sitka Harbor

Starrigavan
Campground
ferry terminal

Halleck
Island

Olga Strait

Krestof
Island

Neva Strait

Krestof
Sound

Point Kaku

Hayward
Point

Kaku
Narrows

Sukoi Inlet

Magoun Islands

Sitka Sound

Sinitsin
Island

Kalinin Bay

Kruzof
Island

Leo Anchorage
Point Leo

Salisbury
Sound

Mt. Edgecumbe

Point Kruzof
Cape Georginia

Klokachef Island
Fortuna Strait

Sea Lion Cove

Cape
Edgecumbe

Kalinin Bay

Before or instead of crossing Salisbury Sound, some kayak-campers choose to spend time in Kalinin Bay, a beautiful reentrant north and west of Sukoi Inlet. Camping here also offers an opportunity to make a day hike to Sea Lion Cove on the outer coast. In settled weather experienced paddlers can visit the cove on a 10-mile day trip. Use caution when rounding Point Kruzof.

continue north toward **Sukoi Inlet**. The pass that leads into Sukoi is negotiable only on higher tides so there is no need to arrive there more than an hour before high water. Once through the pass continue on to Salisbury Sound at **Hayward Point**. It is also possible to make this trip by paddling through **Olga** and **Neva Straits**. However the Krestof-Sukoi route is much more scenic, with far fewer boats and ships or boat wakes to contend with.

At Hayward Point you should make a decision about where to cross Salisbury Sound. In settled weather it is not difficult to cross directly to Chichagof Island from **Sinitsin Island**. A more cautious route can be made by crossing Neva Strait at Hayward Point and continuing north across **Kaku Narrows**. Going this way you mitigate any potential problems of padding through the middle of Salisbury Sound.

Either way you choose to cross Salisbury Sound, the first waypoint you are seeking is **Point Leo** on Chichagof Island. Continuing north from there, the route follows the shoreline to **Khaz Head** on **Khaz Peninsula**. From Point Leo it is 6 miles to **Point Slocum**, then another 3 to **Khaz Point**. Here you'll find some protected water in **Piehle Passage** as you approach Khaz Head. *Caution:* This is open ocean kayaking and should only be undertaken under calm conditions. There are numerous submerged rocks with breakers along this route. Along much of the shore landings are difficult to impossible. On the north side of **Fortuna Strait**, just north of Leo Anchorage, there is an excellent camping spot that is a convenient place to wait for the right conditions before heading north to Khaz Head.

The islands around Khaz Head offer campsites with beautiful views. They can also serve as pleasant base camps for exploring the remote parts of **Slocum Arm**, **Falcon Arm**, and **Ford Arm**. Continuing on north from Khaz Head, those with enough time will want to visit **Klag Bay**, **Lake Anna**, and **Sister Lake**. There is excellent camping throughout this area, and you can go days without seeing another person. Due to the remoteness of the area, wildlife is much more relaxed. You are sure to see plenty of sow brown bears and cubs along the shore as well as river and sea otters, deer, mink, sea lions, and seals. Canada geese and a variety of ducks and gulls are abundant. The abandoned mining town of **Chichagof** at the head of Klag Bay is worth a visit.

Back out on the open coast the **Myriad Islands** are an incredibly beautiful and wild place to camp. Around and among their rocks and islets are vast kelp beds that rise and fall with the ocean swell. Large numbers of sea otters can be seen here, rafts of mothers and kits sunning in the kelp. There is no water available, but campsites are abundant. In calm conditions a trip to the sea lion colony on **White Sisters** is rewarding, but avoid approaching closer than one-quarter mile so as not to disturb the residents.

Continuing northward there is protected paddling to the east of **Herbert Graves Island** and some great exploring in the small bays along the way. **Surveyor Passage** and **Black Bay** are especially charming spots, and there is good camping on the northwest side of **Lydonia Island**. After this you enter **Portlock Harbor** with serene paddling in **Didrickson Bay**, **Pinta Bay**, and especially **Goulding Harbor**. Beyond is fascinating **Dry Pass**, then on into **Little Bay**, where gray whales are commonly present. Just 3 miles beyond Dry Pass is White Sulphur Springs (see Rte. 34). *Farther along:* From the White Sulphur Springs, it is usual to continue on to Pelican, Elfin Cove, Point Adolphus, and then to Hoonah. (Descriptions of these trips are given in Rtes. 34, 35, and 27.)

Appendix 1

Kayak Services in Southeast Alaska

Kayak services in Southeast Alaska are growing, and each year new companies come on the scene. Almost all of the those listed here have been in business for at least two years and some for more than twenty years. The information here is correct as of press time, but please keep in mind that Web sites and e-mail addresses often change. When searching for a specific service on the Internet, start out with the Web site and then try e-mail. If this is not getting you anywhere, try the Web site for the Southeast Alaska town where the business is located. (Those Web sites are listed at the end of this appendix.)

Guided Trips

Gustavus

Spirit Walker Expeditions
This small friendly charter group prides itself on customizing every trip to your interests and time schedule. Spirit Walker specializes in small groups and personal attention. This is an opportunity for a group of friends or a family to kayak together. Customers are provided with an excellent expedition planning guide.
Contact: Spirit Walker Expeditions, P.O. Box 240, Gustavus, AK 99826. Phone: (800) KAYAKER or (907) 697–2266; FAX: (907) 697–2701; e-mail: kayak@he.net; Web site: www.he.net/~kayak.

Haines

Deishu Expeditions
This is a very user-friendly company that has been leading kayak expeditions for seven years. The owner is Haines resident Ned Rozbicki. He and his experienced guides offer a variety of kayaking trips all centered on viewing wildlife, environmental conscience, and the enjoyment of kayaking in beautiful surroundings. Although located in Haines, Ned's excellent trips include other areas in Southeast Alaska.
Contact: Deishu Expeditions, P.O. Box 1406, Haines, AK 99827. Phone: (907) 766–2427 or (800) 552–9257; e-mail: paddle@seakayaks.com; Web site: www.seakayaks.com.

Juneau

Alaska Discovery

Alaska Discovery a well-known and respected company in business since
1972. Alaska Discovery *originated* the idea of guided sea kayak
adventures. The company is run by Ken Leghorn and Sue Warner,
highly experienced Alaska adventurers. Their staff includes more than
forty qualified men and women guides. Alaska Discovery offers more
than one hundred scheduled trips each summer. Most trips are from
three to ten days with eight or ten guests and two guides.
Contact: Alaska Discovery, 5449 Shaune Drive, Suite 4, Juneau, AK
99801. Phone: (800) 586–1911 or (907) 780–6226; FAX: (907)
780–4220; e-mail: akdisco@alaska.net; Web site:
www.gorp.com/akdisc.htm.

Ketchikan

Southeast Exposure

Anyone will enjoy kayaking with Geoff Gross and Betsey Burdett, the
owners of Southeast Exposure. They began this service in 1985. Geoff
and Betsey have led trips for REI and the Sierra Club and are
experienced outdoor adventurers well known for their easy-going, laid-
back kayak trips to Misty Fjords and Prince of Wales Island.
Contact: Southeast Exposure, P.O. Box 9143, 515 Water Street,
Ketchikan, AK 99901. Phone: (907) 225–8829; FAX: (907) 225–8849.

Southeast Sea Kayaks

Greg Thomas and Kim Kirby offer a lot of personalized attention and
assistance to kayakers headed for Misty Fjords, Prince of Wales Island,
and any other Ketchikan-area destinations. In addition to renting kayaks,
they will arrange delivery and pickup transportation, Forest Service
cabin rentals, provisioning, and plenty of advice from their extensive
paddling experience. They have also prepared an excellent *Misty Fjords
Trip Planning Guide* that they sell at a nominal price.
Contact: Southeast Sea Kayaks, P.O. Box 7281, 1430 Millar Street,
Ketchikan, AK 99901. Phone: (800) 287–1607; Phone/Fax: (907)
225–1258; e-mail: bbkayak@ktn.net; Web site: www.ktn.net/seakayaks.

Pelican

Pelican Paddling

Linda Frame and Lindy Dickson started this company in 1997 in an
ideal kayaking location. Pelican Paddling welcomes all kayakers and

Appendix   *-221-*

specializes in families with children who want to experience kayak-camping. Both owners especially enjoy introducing paddlers to native foods that can be gathered from the wild. Linda and Lindy are experienced in the area and know the best places for wildlife viewing in Lisianski Inlet and on the outer coast. **Contact:** Pelican Paddling, P.O. Box 308, Pelican, AK 99823. Phone: (907) 735–2525 or (907) 735–2455; e-mail: kayakak@aol.com; Web site: www.alaskaone.com/pelpaddling.

Petersburg

Tongass Kayak Adventures
Scott Roberge is owner of Tongass Kayak Adventures. He has been kayaking in Alaska for fifteen years, and many people "down south" have attended one of his excellent lectures. His two premier trips are to Le Conte Glacier and to the fascinating Stikine River and Delta. Shorter trips can be arranged. **Contact:** Tongass Kayak Adventures, P.O. Box 2169, Petersburg, AK 99833. Phone: (907) 772–4600; FAX: (907) 722–4646; e-mail: tonkayak@alaska.net; Web site: www.alaska.net/~tonkayak/.

Sitka

Baidarka Boats
Baidarka Boats offers half- and full-day guided trips. (See address under Kayak Rentals.)

Loon Island Sea Kayaking
Loon Island Sea Kayaking includes tours, expeditions, hut-to-hut kayaking, and classes. Owner-operator Scott Brylinsky has been guiding sea kayaking in Southeast Alaska for over sixteen years. A special feature of all of his trips and classes is the recognition and utilization of wild foods of beach and forest. Expeditions of up to seven days are offered. **Contact:** Loon Island Kayaking, P.O. Box 17, Sitka, AK 99835. Phone: (907) 747–8189; e-mail: paddler@ptialaska.net; Web site: www.loon-isl.com.

Sitka Sound Ocean Adventures
Sitka Sound Ocean Adventures is owned by John and Barbara DeLong of Sitka. They have been operating out of their famous Blue Bus at Crescent Harbor since 1994. They offer a variety of half-day, full-day, and week-long guided trips arranged to suit your desires. They can help you arrange for delivery and pickup. **Contact:** Sitka Sound Ocean Adventures, P.O. Box 1242, Sitka, AK 99835. Phone: (907) 747–6375; e-mail: delongb@ptialaska.net; Web site: www.ptialaska.net/~delongb.

Sailing-Kayak Tours

Although the following companies are listed by town, most of them are able to meet you anywhere in Southeast Alaska and arrange a trip to most any place you want to go.

Glacier Bay and Gustavus

Glacier Bay Adventures

The 70-foot *Steller* will take a party of twelve to most any place in the northern part of Southeast Alaska for kayaking and other adventures. Captain Dan Foley has a lot of experience in the area and will pattern the charter to your wishes. Kayaks and all else are furnished. **Contact:** Glacier Bay Adventures, P.O. Box 68, Gustavus, AK 99826. Phone: (907) 697–2442; FAX: (907) 764–2372.

Gustavus Marine Charters

Mike Nigro of Gustavus takes groups of four or six people aboard his 42-foot motor vessel *Kahsteen* on a variety of interesting adventures. For your convenience he brings along double kayaks. Mike also operates a 26-foot C-dory for a kayak transport out of Gustavus and can carry up to six persons and four kayaks. Drop-offs and pickups include Dundas Bay and Yakobi Wilderness. **Contact:** Mike Nigro, P.O. Box 81, Gustavus, AK 99826. Phone: (907) 697–2233; e-mail: gmc@mars.he.net; Web site: www.gustavusmarinecharters.com.

Sea Wolf Wilderness Adventures

The vessel *Sea Wolf* is a fast, comfortable 65-foot cabin cruiser that can accommodate twelve guests. Owner-operators are Rusty Owen and Pamela Miedtke, who are famous for hospitality, outstanding food, and for always knowing where to go for the best kayaking, wildlife viewing, and/or fishing. *Sea Wolf* carries double kayaks for your use. A specialty is kayaking among humpback whales. **Contact:** Sea Wolf Wilderness Adventures, P.O. Box 97, Gustavus, AK 99826. Phone: (907) 697–2416 or (907) 321–1821; e-mail: seawolf_ak@hotmail.com; Web site: www.seawolf-adventures.com.

Wilderness Explorer and Wilderness Adventurer

These two small cruise ships carry thirty-six and seventy-four passengers respectively on four-, five-, and six-day cruises in and near Glacier Bay. Kayaking from the ships is one of several activities offered, and the staff gives instruction and orientation for first-time paddlers. Trips on *Wilderness Explorer* are described as an "active adventure," and those on

Wilderness Adventurer as a "soft adventure." **Contact:** Alaska's Glacier Bay Tours and Charters, 520 Pike Street, Suite 1400, Seattle, WA 98101. Phone: (206) 623–2417 or (800) 451–5952; FAX: (206) 623–7809; e-mail: gbsales@cruisetours.com; Web site: www.glacierbaytours.com.

Pelican

Lisianski Inlet Wilderness Lodge and Charters
The sailing yacht *Demijohn* can take paddlers on overnight trips out of Pelican. (See address under B&Bs Featuring Kayaking.)

Petersburg

Sea Wind Charters
Jim and Kelly Demko will take you on a sailing-kayaking adventure on their 34-foot pilot-house sloop. They furnish the kayaks as well as a comfortable mobile base and will arrange a trip to a variety of fascinating destinations. **Contact:** Sea Wind Charters, P.O. Box 271, Petersburg, AK 99833. Phone: (907) 772–4389; e-mail: seawind@alaska.net; Web site: www.petersburg.org.

Sitka

Moonsong Sailing Expeditions
Moonsong is a 56-foot wood cutter that is ready to take you on whatever kind of sailing-kayaking adventure you want in Southeast Alaska. The crew is Jerry Sharrard and Nola Kathleen, both of whom are experienced sailors and kayakers. Onboard are two double and two single kayaks; *Moonsong* can accommodate up to six persons. **Contact:** Moonsong Sailing Expeditions, P.O. Box 6107, Sitka, AK 99835. Phone: (907) 752–0047; e-mail: sailmoonsong@hotmail.com; Web site: www.alaska.net/~moonsong.

Pacific Expeditions
Skipper Michael Erb is a commercial fisherman who knows the joys of sea kayaking and wants to share them with you. In the summer of 1998, he acquired a flock of new sea kayaks and put them aboard his 74-foot commercial fishing boat *Pacific*. He offers five-day (five-person maximum) expeditions for intermediate and experienced paddlers up and down the west coast of Chichagof Island—one of Southeast Alaska's prime kayaking areas. **Contact:** Pacific Expeditions, P.O. Box 1214, Sitka, AK 99835. Phone: (907) 966–2241; e-mail: kingsway@ptialaska.net; Web site: www.ptialaska.net/~kingsway.

Southeast Alaska Ocean Adventures
Here is an opportunity to live aboard and kayak from the classic 56-foot gaff-rigged cutter *Sequoia*. Owner-operators Noel and Claire Johnson are longtime residents of Southeast Alaska active in commercial fishing. Kayaks are furnished or you can bring your own along. This is a home-style cruise that will appeal especially to those who want a break from the typical tourist glitter. **Contact:** Southeast Alaska Ocean Adventures, P.O. Box 6384, Sitka, AK 99835. Phone: (907) 747–5011.

B&Bs Featuring Kayaking

Elfin Cove

The Hobbit Hole Guesthouse
The Hobbit Hole Guesthouse is a really hidden away place in the Inian Islands, just outside of Elfin Cove. Owners Jane Button and Greg Howe have a new guesthouse and kayaks for guests. The Hobbit Hole is a charming mystical sort of place. **Contact:** The Hobbit Hole Guesthouse, P.O. Box 9, Inian Islands, Elfin Cove, AK 99825. Phone: (907) 723–8514.

South Passage Outfitters
See address under Kayak Rentals.

Juneau

Alaska Discovery
See address under Guided Trips.

Ketchikan

Southeast Sea Kayaks
See address under Guided Trips.

Pelican

Lisianski Inlet Wilderness Lodge and Charters
This well-established lodge places a lot of emphasis on kayaking. Owner Gail Corbin took over this log cabin homestead more than thirty years ago and raised her family here. This is a real get-away-from-it-all place with a lot of paddling opportunities. **Contact:** Lisianski Charters, P.O. Box 765, Pelican, AK 99832. Phone: (907) 735–2266 or (800) 962–8441; e-mail: Kuhook@aol.com; Web site: www.alaskaone.com/starbuck/index.htm.

Otter Cove Bed-and-Breakfast
Otter Cove B&B is the creation of artist Ginnie Porter. It is located on the edge of Pelican in its own tiny cove. Ginnie can arrange kayak trips

and other fascinating activities for you. **Contact:** Otter Cove B&B, P.O.Box 618, Pelican, AK 99832. Phone: (907) 735–2259 or (888) 697–2683; Web site: www.northernlightsdesign.com/ottercove.

Kayak Rental

Elfin Cove

South Passage Outfitters
This family-owned and -operated camp has a tremendous range of options, including cabins, dining room, a yert dormitory, facilities for cooking, and kayak rentals. Owners are Dennis Montgomery and Peggy McDonald. They rent kayaks and camping gear to experienced kayakers. South Passage Outfitters is located at Gull Cove near Elfin Cove. It is a great place for a family kayaking vacation or a place to stop by on the way to and from Point Adolphus. **Contact:** South Passage Outfitters, P.O. Box 48, Elfin Cove, AK 99825. Winter address: 361 Shika Road, Port Townsend, WA 98368. Phone: (360) 385–3417; e-mail: spo@olympus.net; Web site: www.olympus.net/southpass.

Glacier Bay and Gustavus

Glacier Bay Sea Kayaks
This a company of long-standing and solid reputation at Glacier Bay. Included with your rental is an excellent orientation on kayaking safety and techniques, along with advice on camping in Glacier Bay. Personnel are experienced paddlers and can answer your questions on where to go and what to expect during your trip. *Be sure and reserve in advance of your visit.* **Contact:** Glacier Bay Sea Kayaks, P.O. Box 26, Gustavus, AK 99826. Phone: (907) 697–2257, summer: (907) 697–3002; e-mail: kayakak@he.net; Web site: www.he.net/~kayakak/.

Sea Otter Kayaks
Sea Otter Kayaks, operated by Maureen Moore and Ed Bond, is now in its fourth year of serving kayakers in the bay. Before setting out each renter must attend a basic kayak orientation or demonstrate their skills/ experience. Sea Otter can help you with delivery and pickup transportation in Glacier Bay. **Contact:** Sea Otter Kayak, P.O. Box 228, Dock Road, Gustavus, AK 99826. Phone: (907) 697–3007; FAX: 907 697–2338; e-mail: seaotter@he.net; Web site: www.he.net/~seaotter/.

Haines

Deishu Expeditions
See address under Guided Trips.

Juneau

Adventure Sports
This retail store sells and rents bicycles, kayaks, and ski equipment. They can arrange deliveries and pickups for a variety of places on the Juneau road system. Their Web site lists some excellent Juneau area kayak trips. **Contact:** Adventure Sports, 8757 Glacier Highway (Nugget Mall), Juneau, AK 99801. Phone: (907) 789–5696; e-mail: gunnar@alaska.net; Web site: www.adventuresports.com/kayak/seakayak/welcome.htm.

Juneau Outdoor Center
This is a friendly small company with a good reputation. The co-owner and manager is Maridon Boario. The principal business is kayak and kayak equipment rental. Maridon can recommend tours and excursions to fit your schedule. They offer a first-time renter clinic to get you started. Juneau Outdoor Center can arrange delivery and/or pickup transportation for you and your rental kayak to any place on the Juneau road system. **Contact:** Juneau Outdoor Center, P.O. Box 20173, Juneau, AK 99802. Phone: (907) 586–8220; FAX: (907) 586–2575; e-mail: gokayak@alaska.net.

Kayak Express
See address under Kayak Transport Services.

Ketchikan

Southeast Exposure
See address under Guided Trips.

Southeast Sea Kayaks
See address under Guided Trips.

Pelican

Howard Charters
Howard Charters can rent and arrange delivery and pickup services for kayakers in the Pelican area. **Contact:** Howard Charters, P.O. Box 54, Pelican, AK 99832. e-mail: info@howardcharters.com; Web site: www.howardcharters.com.

Kayak Jacks

Kayak Jacks is a new kayak rental business in Pelican. Local managers are Steve and Sheril Young. In the future they expect to have a drop-off and pickup service for paddlers and kayaks. **Contact:** Kayak Jacks, P.O. Box 736, Pelican, AK 99832. Phone: (907) 735–2260; e-mail: akseaplanes.com.

Pelican Paddling

See address under Guided Trips.

Petersburg

Tongass Kayak Adventures

See address under Guided Trips.

Sitka

Baidarka Boats

This respected company was started in 1977 by Larry Edwards, a well-known and -respected kayaker and environmentalist. In addition to rentals Larry is the best source for fiberglass and folding kayaks and kayak equipment in Alaska. His safety requirements for rental kayaks are of the highest standards. **Contact:** Baidarka Boats, 201 Lincoln Street, P.O. Box 6001, Sitka, AK 99835. Phone: (907) 747–8996; FAX: (907) 747–4801; e-mail: 72037.3607@compuserve.com; Web site: execpc.com/~bboats.

Sitka Sound Ocean Adventures

See address under Guided Trips.

Kayak Transport Services

Rates for transporting you and your kayak vary with distance. Get a price quote in advance and be sure you understand if the charge is per person or per trip for several people. Sharing costs among three, four, or more kayakers is the best way to go, and the boat operator may be able to work you in with another group. Some delivery services only do drop-offs and pickups at specific locations. Others will take you any place you want to go.

Elfin Cove

South Passage Outfitters

See address under Kayak Rental.

Gustavus and Northern Southeast Alaska

Cross Sound Express

Skipper Brad Rice and his high speed vessel *Taz* offer kayak and passengers drop-offs and pickups throughout northern Southeast Alaska, including Elfin Cove, Pelican, and the outer coast. He specializes in large groups and can take up to twenty-two passengers. Small groups or individuals can check to see if space is available on other trips. **Contact:** Cross Sound Express, P.O.Box 171, Gustavus, AK 99826. Phone: (907) 697–2726 or (888) 698–2726; e-mail: bhrice@usa.net.

Gustavus Marine Charters

See address under Sailing-Kayak Tours.

Halcyon Charters

Another Gustavus-based boat is operated by Bruce and Karla Tedtsen. Bruce and Karla are experienced boat operators and very knowledgeable about the whales in the area. **Contact:** Halcyon Charters, P.O. Box 153, Gustavus, AK 99826. Phone: (907) 697–2290; FAX: (907) 697–2358.

Mystic Sea Charters

Contact: Mystic Sea Charters, P.O. Box 324, Gustavus, AK 99826. Phone: (800) 699–8422 or (907) 697–2498.

Whale Tale Charters

Contact: Whale Tale Charters, P.O. Box 38, Gustavus, AK 99826. Phone: (907) 697–2286.

Juneau

Adventure Bound

Steve Weber and his 56-foot tour boat *Adventure Bound* make daily sight-seeing trips to Tracy Arm from downtown Juneau (to and within Tracy Arm only). He is always willing to do drop-offs and pickups anywhere in Tracy Arm. Kayaks are launched loaded by lowering with ropes from the *Adventure Bound* deck, and then the paddlers enter their boats via a ladder. Works fine for hardshells, but I don't recommend it for folding boats. **Contact:** Adventure Bound Alaska, P.O. Box 23013, Juneau, AK 99802–3031. Phone: (907) 463–2509 or (800) 228–3875.

Kayak Express

Peter Wright has the oldest delivery/pickup services in Southeast Alaska and a reputation for reliability. He can arrange delivery and pickup any place you want to go on salt water. He also offers kayak rentals, guided day trips, and private base camps with everything furnished. **Contact:** Kayak Express, P.O. Box 210562, Auke Bay, AK 99821. Phone: (907) 790–4591; e-mail: peterb@ptialaska.net; Web site: www.adventuresports.com/asap/kayak/express.

Wilderness Swift Charters
In addition to delivery and pickup services out of Juneau, Andy Romanoff offers some unique camping and boating excursions that can be combined with kayaking. His boat *Wild Abandon* can take up to six passengers with double kayaks. **Contact:** Wilderness Swift Charters, 6205 North Douglas Road, Juneau, AK 99801. Phone: (907) 463–4942; e-mail: tongass@alaska.net; Web site: www.alaska.net/~tongass.

Ketchikan and Southern Southeast Alaska

Alaska Cruises
Kayakers can find transfer services between Ketchikan and Rudyerd Bay in Misty Fjords National Monument with Alaska Cruises. Owner Dale Pihlman has been conducting this service for seventeen years as part of his sight-seeing cruises. He can unload and pickup kayakers at his floating dock at the head of Rudyerd Bay. **Contact:** Alaska Cruises, P.O. Box 7814, 220 Front Street, Ketchikan, AK 99901. Phone: (907) 225–6044 or (800) 228–1905; FAX: (907) 245–8638; e-mail: akcruise@ptialaska.net; Web site: www.ptialaska.net/~akcruise.

Alaskan Aquamarine Experience, Inc.
Johny Gilson and his boat *Experience I* can take you and your kayak anywhere in Misty Fjords and Behm Canal or Prince of Wales Island and arrange to pick you up. **Contact:** Alaskan Aquamarine Experience, Inc., 3857 Fairview, Ketchikan, AK 99901. Phone: (907) 225–2343; Phone/Fax:(907) 225–8886; e-mail: visit@ktn.net; Web site: visit.ktn.net/aae.

Silver King Charters
Don Westlund will drop you off and pick you up anywhere around Revillagigedo Island. His boat can take up to a maximum of six people and six kayaks. Most of his business is into Misty Fjords, but he can suggest some other excellent locations, including Prince of Wales Island. **Contact:** Don Westlund, Silver King Charters, P.O. Box 871, Ward Cove, AK 99928. Phone: (907) 225–9319; FAX: (907) 247–7291.

Pelican

Howard Charters
See address under Kayak Rental.

Lisianski Inlet Cafe Charters
Operated by Victo Stepanenko, who can take or pick up kayaks and paddlers just about anywhere between Juneau and Sitka. Phone: (907) 735–2282.

Lisianski Inlet Wilderness Lodge and Charters
Danny Corbin will take or pick up you and your kayak anywhere you want to go in the area. (See address under B&Bs Featuring Kayaking.)

Petersburg, Wrangell, and Central Southeast Alaska

Sea Wind Charters
See address under Sailing-Kayak Tours.

Tongass Kayak Adventures
See address under Guided Trips.

Sitka

Baidarka Boats
See address under Kayak Rental.

Sitka Sound Ocean Adventures
See address under Guided Trips.

Southeast Alaska Ocean Adventures
See address under Sailing-Kayak Tours.

Ferry Services

Alaska Marine Highway Ferry
The "blue canoes" are the most enjoyable way to get to Southeast Alaska from the Seattle area and to get around within the area. If you are traveling with your own hardshell kayak, it is the best choice. The ferries go to a number of small towns that are convenient locations for starting or ending kayak trips. Reservations are always a good idea, but it is usually possible for "walk-ons" with kayaks to just show up. **Contact:** Alaska Marine Highway System, P.O. Box 25535, Juneau, AK 99802. Phone: (800) 642–0066; FAX: (907) 277–4829; Web site: www.dot.state.ak.us/external/amhs/home.htm.

Auk Nu Ferry

Daily ferry service now operates in the summer between Juneau and Gustavus using a large power catamaran. Transit time is about two and one-half hours. No cars. Limited number of kayaks allowed each trip. Reservations are recommended. **Contact:** Auk Nu Tours, 76 Eagen Drive, Juneau, AK 99801. Phone: (800) 820–2628 or (907) 586–8687; FAX: (907) 586–1337.

Instruction

Alaska Paddle Sports of Juneau

Alaska Paddle Sports is an education-based organization. For beginners there is a full-day hands-on, no nonsense class. Dry suites are furnished, and you will be in and out of your kayak to learn self-rescue and the other basics. The three-day program also teaches wilderness low-impact camping, observing wildlife, how to pack a kayak, crossing techniques, navigation, and dealing with wind, tide, and waves. **Contact:** Alaska Paddle Sports, 800 6th Street, Juneau, AK 99801. Phone: (907) 789–2382; e-mail: akpaddle@eagel.ptialaska.net.

Important Web sites

Gustavus: www.gustavus.com

Haines: www.haines.ak.us/

Juneau: www.juneau.lib.ak.us/jcvb/jcvb.htm

Ketchikan: www.ktn.net/

Petersburg: www.petersburg.org/

Sitka: www.sitka.com

Wrangell: www.wrangell.com

Appendix 2

Cabins & Hiking Trails

U.S. Forest Service Cabins and Shelters Along Kayaking Routes

The U.S. Forest Service maintains 150 cabins and numerous shelters in Southeast Alaska. Some of them are along the routes described in this book. Cabins all have sleeping platforms, wood-burning or oil stoves (you furnish the oil), a counter for food preparation, a table and benches, and an outhouse toilet. All can accommodate four people; some can take larger groups. Three-sided shelters are free and are on a first come basis.

As of 1998 the cabin use fee, which must be paid in advance, is $25 per night. Reservations must also be made in advance. Information on how to rent cabins is available on the Internet at: www.fed.us/r10/chatham/ tnf/recreation/cabins/tnfcabins/htm. This Web site describes each cabin and sometimes includes a photo of the cabin and a location map. Reservations can be made with credit card by mail or by phone: USDA Forest Service Information Center, 101 Egan Drive, Juneau, AK 99801; (907) 586–8751.

Cabins Located Along Kayaking Routes

Routes 3, 5: Jordan Lake, 4.0 miles along Naha Trail from Naha Bay; Hackman Lake, 5.4 miles along Naha Trail from Naha Bay.

Routes 4, 5: Punchbowl (shelter), 0.9 mile on trail from Punchbowl Cove; Manzanita Bay (shelter); Checats, 1.1 miles along Checats Cove Trail from Checats Bay; Alava Bay.

Route 5: Plenty Cutthroat, 1.2 miles along Orchard Bay Trail from Shrimp Bay; Blind Pass; Anchor Pass; Shelokum Lake (shelter), 2.2 miles from Baily Bay on Shelokum Trail.

Route 6: The following cabins are on the Stikine River: Mount Flemar, Mount Rynda, Sakes Slough 1 and 2, Twin Lakes. The following cabins are on the Stikine River Delta: Binkley Slough, Gut Island 1 and 2, Koknuk, Sergief, Little Dry Island, Mallard Slough.

Route 8: Beecher Pass, Kah Sheets Bay, Devils Elbow, and Big John Bay.

Route 11: Berners Bay.

Route 25: Salt Lake Bay.
Route 33: Greentop Harbor.

Route 34: White Sulpher Springs.

Route 40: Allan Point.

State of Alaska Cabins Along Kayaking Routes

As of 1998 charges for the state of Alaska cabin use is $25 per night. For specific information on the Web: nutmeg.state.ak.us/ixpress/dnr/ parks/south.dml. Mailing address is Southwest Area Office, 400 Willoughby Avenue, 4th Floor, Juneau, AK 99801; (907) 465–4563.

Route 11: Cowee Meadows Cabin, Point Bridget State Park.

Route 13: Seymour Canal Cabin at the south end of tramway between Oliver Inlet and Seymour Canal.

Forest Service Hiking Trails

There are some hiking trails that can be reached by kayak. The following is a Web site listing hiking trails maintained by the U.S. Forest Service in Southeast Alaska:
www.fed.us/r10/chatham/tnf/recreation/trails/hiking.htm.

You can also obtain hiking trail information by writing to the USDA Forest Service Information Center, 101 Egan Drive, Juneau, AK 99801; (907) 586–8751. The Forest Service also has walk-in visitor centers in Juneau, Ketchikan, and Sitka.

Appendix 3

Kayaking Maps for Southeast Alaska

The two most commonly used kayaking maps are USGS topographic maps and NOAA nautical charts. United States Geological Survey (USGS) topographic maps put the emphasis on the topography; the waterways are of secondary importance. National Oceanographic and Atmospheric Administration (NOAA) charts are marine maps and put the emphasis on the waterways and shorelines. Hence topography is secondary. Note that by convention land maps are usually referred to as topographic or topo maps, whereas nautical maps are called charts. There are also some special Forest Service kayak maps for use in Southeast Alaska.

USGS Topographic Maps

Most topographic maps of Southeast Alaska are either at the scale of 1:250,000 or 1:63,360. For kayaking 1:250,000 scale maps may be sufficient, but they lack the kind of detail you often prefer. A scale of 1:63,360 is OK, but the maps only cover an area of about 210 square miles, which means you have to haul many maps for some trips.

Topo maps can be ordered using a credit card by calling 1–800–435–6277. If you don't know the specific map you need, you can call that number and request an Alaska index map, which will be sent to you without charge and from which you can prepare a map order.

NOAA Charts

Marine charts are more expensive than topographic maps, but they are often more useful for sea kayaking. They are printed on better quality paper and will outlast topographic maps. The scale of NOAA charts is often more convenient than that used on topo maps. For example, a lot of NOAA charts are at a scale of 1:40,000 and 1:80,000. NOAA charts have the added advantage of showing navigation aids and providing important water safety information not included on topographic maps.

NOAA charts can often be purchased from local chart dealers. But unless you are in Alaska, dealers will usually have to order them, and these days you can do this just as easily yourself.

You can request a free Alaska NOAA catalog by calling 1–800–638–8975. With a credit card you can order NOAA charts by e-mail through the NOAA Web site: 140.90.115.75/ordercharts.htm. Charts can also be ordered by phone or mail from NOAA Distribution Division, N/ACC3, National Ocean Service, Riverdale, MD 20737–1199, or by phone using the 800 number or by FAX at (301) 436–6829.

Forest Service Canoe & Kayak Maps

The Forest Service maps are useful, but they are printed on poor quality paper—be sure to use them with a sealable map sleeve. For information about Forest Service maps try their Web site: www.fs.fed.us/r10/chatham/tnf/publications/maps.htm.

You will find the following maps useful for the trips listed:

Route 6: *Stikine River* ($4.00) for use up to the Canadian Border.

Route 8: *Kuiu Island* ($4.00).

Routes 3, 4, and 5: *Misty Fjords Monument Map* ($4.00). Although this map scale is 1:250,000, you can get by with it alone for the trips indicated. It also shows the location of U.S. Forest Service cabins and shelters.

These maps can be ordered by mail or by phone with credit card from Forest Service Information Center, 101 Egan Drive, Juneau, AK 99801; (907) 586–8751. Make checks payable to Alaska Natural History Association (ANHA).

Canadian Topographic Maps

Anyone paddling the Canadian part of the Stikine River will want to obtain the appropriate topographic maps. Canadian topos are made at a scale of 1:50,000 and 1:250,000. The Web site maps.NRCan.gc.ca/cmo/dealers.html lists map agents in the United States and Canada who handle the maps you need.

Copies & Care

Because charts and maps are expensive, some people choose to make photocopies. Unfortunately photocopy paper is seldom of very good quality, and if the maps get wet, they will be useless. The option is to laminate them or treat the paper with a waterproofing material sold in most outdoor recreation stores. Waterproofing works well on topo maps. I don't know if it works on photocopies. With any kind of map a sealable transparent map sleeve or envelope is absolutely necessary. All outfitters offer them for sale.

Appendix 4

Worthwhile Reading

Adventure Kayaking—Trips in Glacier Bay, Don Skillman, 1988, Wilderness Press, Berkeley, CA, 154 pp. *Excellent up-to-date guide to trips within Glacier Bay.*

Alaska: A Lonely Planet Travel Survival Kit, Jim DuFresne, 1997, Lonely Planet Publications, Oakland, CA, 449 pp. *An excellent planning guide with tons of important information. You will probably want to remove the Southeast Alaska section and take it along on your trip.*

Alaska's Southeast: Touring the Inside Passage, Sara Eppenbach, 1997, Globe Pequot Press, Old Saybrook, CT, 344 pp. *Excellent no-nonsense look at the cities, towns, and characteristics of Southeast Alaska.*

Alaska-Yukon Handbook, Deke Castleman and Don Pitcher, 1997, Moon Publications, Chico, CA, 498 pp. *Another excellent planning guide with the details on lodging and restaurants.*

Backcountry Bear Basics, Dave Smith, 1997, The Mountaineers, Seattle, WA, 110 pp. *A "must read" for everyone planning to kayak-camp in Southeast Alaska.*

Discovering Wild Plants: Alaska, Western Canada, the Northwest, Janice J. Schofield, 1992, Alaska Northwest Books, Anchorage, 354 pp. *Somewhat large and heavy to take along but an outstanding guide. Especially valuable for those who want to use as many plants as possible for food.*

Glacier Bay National Park, Jim DuFresne, 1987, The Mountaineers, Seattle, WA, 152 pp. *An excellent guide to kayaking in Glacier Bay.*

Guide to the Birds of Alaska, Robert H. Armstrong, 1995, Alaska Northwest Books, Anchorage, 322 pp. *This is a book I always take with me when kayaking.*

The Nature of Southeast Alaska, Rita O'Clair, Robert H. Armstrong, and R. Carstensen, 1997, Graphic Arts Center, Portland, OR, 255 pp. *A top-notch, fact-filled nature guide to Southeast Alaska. Be sure to read it before you go.*

Plants of the Pacific Northwest Coast: Washington, Oregon, British Columbia, and Alaska, Jim Pojar and Andy MacKinnon, eds., 1994, Lone Pine Publishing, Redmond, WA, 528 pp. *Another book that goes with me when kayaking. OK, it is sort of heavy, but it is also indispensible if you want to know the vegetation.*

Travels in Alaska, John Muir, 1988, Sierra Club Books, San Francisco, CA, 274 pp. *A book you are sure to enjoy from Muir's travels to Southeast Alaska over 100 years ago (without Gore-Tex, freeze-dried foods, or guidebooks).*

Wildlife Notebook Series, Cheryl Hull, ed., 1994, Alaska Department Fish and Game, Juneau. *Excellent concise summary of the most common Alaska wildlife.*

Appendix 5

Miscellaneous Addresses

Glacier Bay National Park and Preserve
P.O. Box 140
Gustavus, AK 99826
Phone: (907) 697–2230
E-mail: glba_adminstration@nps.gov
Web site: www.nps.gov/glba/

Misty Fjords National Monument
3031 Tongass Avenue
Ketchikan, AK 99901
Phone: (907) 225–2148

Tongass National Forest
USDA Forest Service Information Center
101 Egan Drive
Juneau, AK 99801
Phone: (907) 586–8751

Index

A

B

C

Index